1000
Fire- Packed Thanksgiving Prayers to Crush Sickness and Defeat the Devil

Unstoppable Declarations of Healing, wholeness, long life, and supernatural victory

Second Edition

Copyright & Rights

© 2025 Tracy C. Moonga. All rights reserved.
No part of this publication may be reproduced, transmitted, stored in a retrieval system, or shared in any form or by any means—whether photocopying, electronic, recording, or otherwise—without the prior written permission of the author.

Unauthorized reproduction, distribution, or transmission is strictly prohibited unless authorized by the Author of this book.

Dedication

I dedicate this book to my Heavenly Father, the Lord God Almighty, the Great Healer, and the Giver of life.

All glory, honor, and praise belong to You forever.

I also dedicate this work to every soul who desires to experience divine healing, total restoration, and the abundant life promised through Jesus Christ.

May your healing spring forth speedily, and may you walk in divine health all the days of your life.

Message to the Reader

Beloved, this is not just a book — it is fire in your hands!

This is a spiritual weapon for healing, restoration, and the manifestation of long life.

Use it daily — consistently, seriously, and with commitment.

Speak these thanksgiving prayers with faith, boldness, and confidence.

Whether you are sick, healed, or simply seeking to live a long, strong life — this book is for you.

There is no sickness that God cannot heal.

There is no incurable disease that cannot bow at the name of Jesus.

With God, all things are possible! (Matthew 19:26)

This book will help you rise above sickness, disease, oppression, depression, and fear — into the abundant life Jesus paid for at the Cross!

You need this book at all times — at the mountaintop or in the valley — because the Word of God is life, health, medicine, and strength for every season of life.

How to Use This Book Daily

You can read:

250 prayers at morning

250 prayers at lunchtime (12:00 pm)

250 prayers at 4:00 pm

250 prayers at 7:00 pm

250 prayers at 12:00 midnight

OR

500 prayers in the morning

500 prayers in the afternoon

500 prayers at 6:00 pm

500 prayers at midnight

And at the end of each prayer session, take Communion!

Be consistent. Be aggressive in the spirit.

Be serious.

This is FIRE.

There is no sickness that God cannot heal.

Communion Verses to Read Before Taking the Lord's Supper

1 Corinthians 11:23–26

John 6:53–58

Isaiah 53:5

1 Peter 2:24

Prayer Before Taking Communion

Heavenly Father,

I come before You with reverence and gratitude.

Thank You for the broken body and shed blood of Jesus Christ.

As I partake of this Communion, I discern the body of Christ, and I receive divine healing, strength, and restoration.

I plead the blood of Jesus over my body, soul, and spirit.

I eat and drink today for life, healing, wholeness, and victory.

In Jesus› mighty name, Amen.

Prayer After Taking Communion

Father,

Thank You for this Holy Communion.

I receive all the benefits of the finished work of Christ:

Healing in my body

Restoration in my soul

Eternal life in my spirit

I am healed. I am restored. I am redeemed.

Thank You, Jesus!

Hallelujah! Amen.

Why Confessing God's Word Is Powerful

The Word of God is alive. It is spirit and it is life (John 6:63).

When you confess the Word, you release creative power into your atmosphere, into your body, and into your future.

Life and death are in the power of the tongue (Proverbs 18:21).

Faith comes by hearing, and hearing by the Word of God (Romans 10:17).

The Word of God is medicine to all your flesh (Proverbs 4:20–22).

Confessing God's Word daily builds your faith, renews your mind, strengthens your body, and aligns you with Heaven's promises. Never underestimate the power of speaking the Word! Speak it until you see it! Speak it until your life becomes the manifestation of God's promises!

Salvation Prayer

If you have not yet given your life to Jesus Christ, pray this prayer sincerely now

Lord Jesus,

I believe You are the Son of God. I believe You died for my sins and rose again on the third day.

Today, I confess You as my Lord and Saviour.

Forgive me of all my sins. Wash me with Your blood.

Fill me with Your Holy Spirit.

Write my name in the Book of Life.

From today, I am born again, saved, redeemed, and set free! In Jesus' name, Amen!

Welcome to the family of God!

Now you can begin using this book daily — as a child of God, redeemed by the blood of Jesus!

1000 Thanksgiving Prayers for Divine Healing, Long Life, and Total Restoration

1.

Jesus, Commander of Fire, I thank You for releasing judgment on every demonic root hiding in my nervous system!

(Nahum 1:6)

Let the strongholds crumble by the breath of fire!

2.

Holy One of Israel, I thank You that every bloodline curse is incinerated by the altar of Your holiness!

(Isaiah 10:17)

Let the fire of holiness replace family affliction!

3.

The One Who Makes All Things New, I thank You that organs, tissues, bones, and glands are now under divine reconstruction!

(Revelation 21:5)

Let the blueprint of Heaven overwrite human error!

4.

Jesus, the Flame in My Bones, I thank You for setting my entire being ablaze with incorruptible health!

(Jeremiah 20:9)

Let my immune system burn with Holy Ghost voltage!

5.

Yahweh Tsabaoth, Lord of Hosts, I thank You that every demon of affliction is arrested and chained in eternal fire!

(Jude 1:6)

Let the captors become captives!

6.

The Finger That Wrote on Stone, I thank You that You have engraved healing into my very DNA!

(Exodus 31:18)

No disease can edit what Heaven wrote!

7.

The Fire-Wrapped God, I thank You that I am surrounded by a glory circle — no attack can enter!

(Zechariah 2:5)

I am not exposed — I am encased in flame!

8.

Jesus, My Stronghold, I thank You that symptoms are now prisoners and I am the free man walking out of the fire!

(Daniel 3:26)

Let every chain drop into the fire pit!

9.

The Storm-Rider, I thank You that even storms obey You — so every medical storm now bows to Your Word!

(Mark 4:39)

Let the storm be silenced by one word: "HEALED!"

10.

Elohei Marom, God of Heights, I thank You for lifting me so high that affliction can't reach me anymore!

(Psalm 148:13)

Let my enemies stretch and still fail!

11.

Jesus, the Warrior Lamb, I thank You that the same Lamb who died now fights for me with fire in His eyes!

(Revelation 5:6)

Slain Lamb — now roaring Lion!

12.

Jehovah Shammah, the God Who is Present, I thank You for entering my sickroom and driving out every unclean spirit!

(Mark 1:25–27)

Your presence makes affliction illegal!

13.

El Rachum, the Compassionate God, I thank You for healing me not just because I'm righteous — but because You are good!

(Psalm 145:8)

Mercy rewrote my medical history!

14.

Jesus, the Fiery Judge, I thank You for executing vengeance on the strongman behind lingering symptoms!

(Psalm 94:1)

Let justice fall like fire on every altar of pain!

15.

The Living Sacrifice, I thank You for taking my place in judgment — now I rise in perfect peace!

(Isaiah 53:4–5)

Let divine exchange speak louder than symptoms!

16.

Alpha of My Healing, I thank You for beginning a story that hell can't edit, delay, or reverse!

(Philippians 1:6)

I'm not waiting to be healed — it already began in glory!

17.

Jesus, the Man of Sorrows, I thank You that You bore the very pain the enemy said would finish me!

(Isaiah 53:3–4)

You took it — I don't take it again!

18.

The Sword-Wielding Savior, I thank You for slicing off inherited infirmity and replacing it with divine inheritance!

(Ephesians 1:11)

I inherit wholeness — nothing less!

19.

The Voice of Many Waters, I thank You that Your Word drowns every voice of fear, pain, and defeat!

(Revelation 1:15)

Let every whisper of hell be washed away!

20.

The Commander of Whirlwinds, I thank You that every satanic plan has been scattered like chaff in a storm!

(Psalm 83:13–15)

Let the whirlwind of Yahweh clean the atmosphere!

21

The Inextinguishable Light, I thank You that no shadow of disease can coexist with the light You've placed in me!

(John 1:5)

Let there be unrelenting light in every cell!

22.

The Covenant-Maker, I thank You that Your Word is not a suggestion — it's a legal binding fire-sealed promise!

(Psalm 89:34)

Let the covenant cancel every contradiction!

23.

Jesus, the Word Sent, I thank You that Your Word entered my bloodstream and rewrote the script!

(Psalm 107:20)

No sentence can resist the scroll from Heaven!

24.

The Architect of Glory, I thank You that my frame is now aligned with Heaven's original blueprint — perfect health!

(Psalm 139:14–16)

Let divine design manifest without resistance!

25.

Jesus, my Deliverer, I thank You that You pulled me from the pit of slow decay and placed me in the fast lane of recovery!

(Psalm 40:2)

Let resurrection speed cancel every delay!

26.

El Gibbor, Mighty Warrior, I thank You that You are tearing down the walls of every stubborn infirmity by force!

(Isaiah 9:6)

No resistance shall stand before Your charge!

27.

The Living Flame, I thank You that my entire bloodstream is baptized in fire — sickness cannot survive this heat!

(Isaiah 66:15)

Let divine fire surge through every cell!

28.

Jesus, the Master of Time, I thank You for redeeming lost years of health — I recover it all, with interest!

(Joel 2:25)

What I lost in pain, I gain in power!

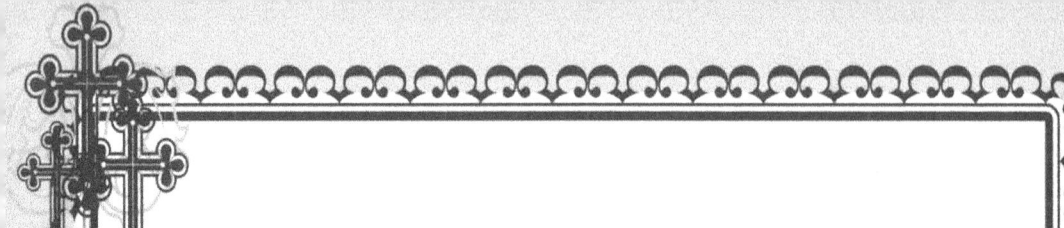

29.

Jehovah Tsidkenu, my Righteousness, I thank You that affliction has no case against my righteous identity!

(Jeremiah 23:6)

I am justified — let affliction be disqualified!

30.

The All-Knowing God, I thank You that You diagnosed what doctors missed and corrected what man could not!

(Hebrews 4:13)

Let divine insight override human ignorance!

31.

The One Who Wounds and Heals, I thank You that what You cut out, You now replace with glory!

(Deuteronomy 32:39)

Every pain You removed makes room for power!

32.

El Elyon, the Most High, I thank You that no low place of affliction can compete with Your elevation of my health!

(Psalm 91:1)

I'm too lifted to be afflicted again!

33.

Jesus, My Reward, I thank You that because I believe, I now receive — no delay, no denial, no defeat!

(Hebrews 11:6)

My healing is a reward sealed in fire!

34.

The Revealer of Mysteries, I thank You for exposing the root behind the symptom and uprooting it forever!

(Daniel 2:22)

Let the axe strike where it matters most!

35.

Jesus, the Resurrected One, I thank You that even things I forgot to pray about have been healed by Your mercy!

(Romans 8:26)

Your Spirit covered what my words missed!

36.

The Lord My Shield, I thank You that demonic arrows now ricochet and return to sender — sevenfold!

(Psalm 91:5–7)

Let the fire of immunity stand forever!

37.

The Restorer of Years, I thank You for returning what sickness tried to steal — time, strength, confidence, and voice!

(Joel 2:25)

**Let divine restoration thunder over

38.

Jehovah-Makkeh, the Lord who strikes, I thank You for striking down the altars where sickness was programmed!

(Ezekiel 7:9)

Let the altar crash under judgment fire!

39.

Jesus, my Eternal Covering, I thank You that no strange fire, spell, or incantation can land on my body!

(Numbers 23:23)

My covering is blood — my defense is flame!

40.

The Word Made Flesh, I thank You that every spoken promise has now taken physical form in my life!

(John 1:14)

Let Your Word be seen in my bones!

41.

The One Who Rolled the Stone, I thank You that every stone of delay, death, and hindrance is permanently moved!

(John 11:39–44)

My grave has no grip — I've stepped out in glory!

42.

The Oil from Heaven, I thank You that every dry place is now drenched with power, healing, and overflow!

(Isaiah 10:27)

No dryness survives Your anointing!

43.

The God Who Calls Things Forth, I thank You for calling my cells, my breath, my heart, and my strength back into alignment!

(Romans 4:17)

Let alignment obey Your voice!

44.

The One Enthroned in Fire, I thank You that no darkness can occupy where Your throne is established!

(Psalm 97:2–5)

Let every squatters' spirit be burned out now!

45.

The God Who Does Wondrous Things, I thank You that what no man could do — You have done in one breath!

(Psalm 72:18)

Let the glory point back to You alone!

46.

Jesus, my Resurrection Banner, I thank You that my life waves victory after what tried to bury me!

(John 11:25)

This flag of triumph shall fly forever!

47.

The Lightning of Heaven, I thank You for striking down sickness with speed, force, and finality!

(Luke 10:18)

Let every demonic nest be split by lightning!

48.

The Builder of Broken Walls, I thank You that the wall of defense around my health is now reinforced with fire!

(Nehemiah 2:17)

Let breaches be rebuilt with holy bricks!

49.

The Lamb Who Was Slain, I thank You that the sacrifice of Jesus settled my case forever — no reversal, no appeal!

(Revelation 5:9)

Let Calvary speak louder than symptoms!

50.

The One Who Holds the Scroll, I thank You that the book of my life is sealed with healing, not tragedy!

(Revelation 5:1–5)

Let Heaven's script override Earth's report!

51.

The Voice Like a Trumpet, I thank You for blasting away every veil that blocked my full healing!

(Revelation 1:10)

Let trumpet fire tear every dark canopy!

52.

Jesus, my Confidence, I thank You that I don't fear relapse, recurrence, or return — it is FINISHED!

(John 19:30)

Let the seal of completion rest on me forever!

53.

The Flame of the Altar, I thank You that Your fire is now my defense system — automatic, aggressive, unquenchable!

(Leviticus 6:13)

Let fire on my altar burn without apology!

54.

The Warrior with the Sword, I thank You that You have pierced through the stubborn spirit behind long-term torment!

(Hebrews 4:12)

Let Your sword divide and destroy every root!

55.

Jehovah Rohi, my Shepherd, I thank You that You've led me out of valleys, out of fear, and into restoration!

(Psalm 23:1–3)

Let green pastures surround me in peace!

56.

Jesus, my Immovable Rock, I thank You that my body is now built on unshakable promises — no more cycles, no more crashes!

(Psalm 62:2)

Let divine stability become my new normal!

57.

The Finisher of My Healing, I thank You that You don't do partial work — I receive wholeness, totality, and overflow!

(Philippians 1:6)

Let my testimony be stamped "complete in Christ!"

58.

The Breaker of Patterns, I thank You for permanently deleting recurring symptoms and dismantling evil cycles!

(Nahum 1:9)

Let what kept returning be buried forever!

59.

The Voice in My Wilderness, I thank You for guiding me out of diagnostic deserts into rivers of restoration!

(Isaiah 43:19)

Let glory spring up where despair used to grow!

60.

My Father, my God, I thank You that my body is now too fire-filled for any stranger to inhabit again!

(1 Corinthians 6:19)

Let holiness electrify every cell within me!

61.

The Owner of My Body, I thank You for evicting every illegal tenant from my organs, blood, and bones!

(Psalm 24:1)

This temple belongs to You — permanently!

62.

Jesus, the One Who Paid It All, I thank You that I owe no more pain — You paid in full with Your blood!

(1 Peter 2:24)

Let no demon send another bill!

63.

The King of Clean Slates, I thank You for giving me a brand-new record — no past labels, no inherited curses, no medical shame!

(Colossians 2:14)

Let the eraser of Heaven wipe out every old script!

64.

The Restorer of Breath, I thank You for filling my lungs with supernatural oxygen — every breath declares life!

(Job 33:4)

Let my breath become praise and power!

65.

The Banner Over Me, I thank You for covering me with the flag of victory — no defeat, no delay, no decay!

(Song of Solomon 2:4)

Let my healing fly high as Your testimony!

66.

The Giver of Days, I thank You for adding years to my life, and life to my years!

(Proverbs 3:1–2; Psalm 91:16)

Let long life be loud with glory!

67

The Fire on My Tongue, I thank You that every word I speak carries life, power, and irreversible results!

(Proverbs 18:21)

Let my confessions create what You promised!

68.

The God of No Expiry, I thank You that my healing is not seasonal — it is forever, backed by eternity!

(Hebrews 13:8)

Let permanent fire dwell in my testimony!

69.

Jesus, the Word Sent to Me, I thank You that the Word didn't return void — it accomplished healing with fire!

(Isaiah 55:11)

Let fulfilled prophecy walk through my veins!

70.

My Fire Wall, I thank You that I am surrounded by Holy Ghost flames — day and night, home and abroad!

(Zechariah 2:5)

Let no arrow cross the bloodline of fire!

71.

The One Who Numbers My Hairs, I thank You for caring so deeply that not even microscopic damage escapes Your attention!

(Luke 12:7)

Let personalized healing cover every detail!

72.

The One Who Walks in the Fire, I thank You for entering my furnace and rewriting my outcome!

(Daniel 3:25)

Let fire fight fire — until glory rises!

1073.

Jehovah Rebuilder, I thank You for reconstructing every torn place with heavenly materials — stronger than ever!

(Isaiah 61:4)

Let divine architecture replace human repairs!

74.

Jesus, the Anchor of My Health, I thank You for anchoring me in faith, fire, and full recovery!

(Hebrews 6:19)

Let no wave shake this fire-secured foundation!

75.

The One Who Never Sleeps, I thank You for working behind the scenes while I rested — I woke up stronger!

(Psalm 121:3–4)

Let glory work while I worship and sleep!

76.

The Light in My Bones, I thank You that every trace of darkness has been exposed and exiled by Your brilliance!

(Proverbs 4:22)

Let illumination flush out every hidden threat!

77.

The Restorer of Strength, I thank You that fatigue and weakness are over — I run and do not grow weary!

(Isaiah 40:31)

Let eagle-level strength rise without delay!

78.

Jesus, the Destroyer of Yokes, I thank You for demolishing the chains that once held me captive to cycles of sickness!

(Isaiah 10:27)

Let every yoke be shattered beyond repair!

79.

The Caller of Destinies, I thank You for calling me out of affliction and into fire-soaked purpose!

(1 Peter 2:9)

Let my voice echo louder than my past pain!

80.

The River That Heals, I thank You that wherever You flow, dead things live again — flow through me now!

(Ezekiel 47:9)

Let my entire being drink from Your stream!

81.

The Lifter of Shame, I thank You that the stigma of affliction has been swallowed by a flood of glory!

(Isaiah 61:7)

Let celebration replace medical humiliation!

82.

The Healer of Generations, I thank You that what my parents suffered — I overcome by fire!

(Psalm 112:2)

Let it stop with me — and glory begin!

83.

The Final Authority, I thank You that no lab result, no file, and no report has the final say — You do!

(Isaiah 46:10)

Let Your verdict of victory stand forever!

84.

The One Who Opens Wombs and Paths, I thank You for opening what no man could open — in body, spirit, and future!

(Genesis 30:22; Isaiah 45:2)

Let opening season never end in my life!

85.

Jesus, My Sure Foundation, I thank You that no shaking can dislodge the healing You've established in me!

(Isaiah 28:16)

Let my roots grow deep in divine health!

86.

The Mighty One of Israel, I thank You for roaring over my bloodline and cleansing every spiritual pollution!

(Isaiah 1:24–26)

Let holy fire run through my ancestry!

87.

The Master of Completion, I thank You for finishing every unfinished area of my healing — no half victories!

(Ecclesiastes 3:14)

Let the full package of wholeness manifest now!

88.

The One Who Seals, I thank You for stamping my healing with fire, blood, and finality — no reversal!

(Ephesians 1:13)

Let Your seal break every enemy attempt to return!

89.

The God Who Celebrates, I thank You that You rejoice over me with singing — I now dance with divine energy!

(Zephaniah 3:17)

Let Heaven's joy overflow into my strength!

90.

Jesus, My Safe Place, I thank You for hiding me in glory until every storm passed — I rise untouched!

(Psalm 27:5)

Let divine shelter become daily reality!

91.

The One Who Satisfies, I thank You that I'm not just healed — I'm full, refreshed, and running over!

(Psalm 23:5)

Let my life spill glory everywhere!

92.

The Defender of Fire Carriers, I thank You that because I burn for You, hell can't burn me!

(Luke 24:32)

Let passion be my preservation!

93.

Jesus, the Flame Between Me and Danger, I thank You for standing between me and every affliction that tried to return!

(Numbers 16:48)

Let fire form a line the enemy cannot cross!

94.

The One Who Wrote My Name, I thank You that my name is written in the Book of Life, not in the charts of death!

(Luke 10:20)

Let eternal health be my inheritance!

95.

The One Who Took My Place, I thank You that You were pierced so I could dance again!

(Isaiah 53:5)

Let every stripe birth supernatural strength!

96.

The Strength of Zion, I thank You that my recovery is now accelerated beyond human timelines!

(Isaiah 66:7–9)

Let what takes years be done in days!

97.

The All-Consuming God, I thank You that this fire shall not fade — it will guard me forever!

(Hebrews 12:29)

Let fire be my atmosphere from now on!

98.

Jesus, My Divine Insurance, I thank You that no unexpected evil shall hijack my health, my home, or my destiny!

(Psalm 91:10–11)

Let my coverage be unbreakable!

99.

The One Who Leads Me in Triumph, I thank You that every sickness I defeated becomes a testimony I carry into nations!

(2 Corinthians 2:14)

Let my story shake hell and glorify Heaven!

100.

Father, I thank You!

You turned my valley into a furnace, my tears into weapons, my pain into praise, and my battle into legacy.

From this point forward — no sickness, no delay, no fear, no return.

This body is Yours. This fire is Yours. This victory is Yours. Forever.

In Jesus' mighty name —

AMEN!

101.

El Elyon, God Most High, I thank You for lifting me above the grip of affliction — I soar while sickness sinks!
(Psalm 91:1)

Hallelujah! You are higher than every report!

102.

Jesus, the Word of God, I thank You that Your Word didn't just speak — it performed surgery inside me!
(Hebrews 4:12)

Praise be to God! Your Word healed me!

103.

Jehovah Nissi, my Banner, I adore You for waving victory over my life while the enemy watched and wept!
(Exodus 17:15)

You are greater than the greatest! My banner is fire!

104.

Emmanuel, God With Us, I thank You for never abandoning me in the storm — You walked me out of it!
(Isaiah 43:2)

Hallelujah! I came out without smoke on me!

105.

Jesus, the Great Intercessor, I thank You for praying for me when I couldn't pray — and snatching me back from the edge!

(Luke 22:32; Hebrews 7:25)

Praise be to God! My testimony is proof of Your mercy!

106.

The Bright Morning Star, I adore You for shining into my darkest place — You broke the night and ushered in glory!

(Revelation 22:16)

Hallelujah! Darkness had to bow!

107.

El Roi, the God who sees me, I thank You for watching when no one else noticed and acting when no one else could!

(Genesis 16:13)

God I adore You! You see, You care, You heal!

108.

The Root of David, I thank You for rooting me in strength and fruitfulness after years of barrenness!

(Revelation 5:5)

You are greater than the greatest, Jesus!

109.

Jehovah Rapha, my Healer, I praise You for burning out every diagnosis with holy vengeance!

(Exodus 15:26)

Praise be to God — healing is my inheritance!

110.

Jesus, the Author and Finisher of My Faith, I thank You for finishing what the enemy tried to interrupt!

(Hebrews 12:2)

Hallelujah! The fire wrote the last chapter!

111.

The God Who Makes Rivers in the Desert, I thank You for opening supernatural healing paths where man said "no way!"

(Isaiah 43:19)

Praise be to God! You made a way in my body!

112.

Jesus, the Lamb and the Lion, I adore You for being my sacrifice and my warrior — You bled, then roared!

(Revelation 5:5–6)

God, You are greater than the greatest! Hallelujah!

113.

The Consuming Fire, I thank You for igniting an inferno in my life — nothing unclean can dwell here again!

(Hebrews 12:29)

Let Your fire keep burning! I adore You, my Holy Flame!

114.

Jehovah Jireh, the Provider, I thank You for providing healing I didn't deserve and peace I couldn't buy!

(Genesis 22:14)

Hallelujah! You paid what I couldn't!

115.

Jesus, the Resurrection and the Life, I thank You for calling me out of medical graves and giving me back my voice!

(John 11:25)

Praise be to God — dead things rose!

116.

El Shaddai, the All-Sufficient God, I thank You that You didn't need help to heal me — You alone are more than enough!

(Genesis 17:1)

You are greater than the greatest, El Shaddai!

117.

Jesus, the Anchor of My Soul, I adore You for holding me steady while the storm tried to sink me!

(Hebrews 6:19)

God I adore You! I'm still here because of You!

118.

Jehovah Tsabaoth, Lord of Hosts, I thank You for dispatching angel armies to destroy every demonic health agenda!

(2 Kings 6:17)

Praise be to God — I live in a fire zone!

119.

The Faithful Witness, I thank You for testifying in Heaven that "this one shall live and not die!"

(Revelation 1:5)

Hallelujah! Heaven agrees — I shall live!

120.

The Lion of Judah, I adore You for roaring over my bones, my breath, and my blood — and silencing the grave!

(Amos 3:8; Revelation 5:5)

Let the roar of victory echo forever — You are greater than the greatest!

121.

El Olam, Everlasting God, I thank You that my life is not short-changed — I will live to declare Your wonders!

(Psalm 118:17)

Hallelujah! I shall not die, I shall testify!

122.

Jesus, the Lengthener of Days, I thank You that my years are not being stolen — You are multiplying them with joy!

(Proverbs 3:1–2)

Praise be to God! You are greater than the grave!

123.

The Fountain of Life, I adore You for saturating my bones, blood, and breath with the river of renewal!

(Psalm 36:9)

God I adore You — I drink from the well of fire!

124.

The Rock of Ages, I thank You for making my life untouchable by plagues and unstoppable by time!

(Isaiah 26:4)

Let long life glorify You, Lord!

125.

Jehovah Rapha, I praise You that You didn't just touch me — You completed the work and sealed me whole!

(Exodus 15:26)

Hallelujah! I am healed forever!

126.

The One Who Renews My Youth, I thank You that age cannot steal my strength — I soar like an eagle!

(Psalm 103:5)

You are greater than the greatest, my Glory Restorer!

127.

Jesus, my Resurrection, I thank You that old age shall not mean decline — it will mean deeper fire!

(Isaiah 46:4)

God I adore You — even in my grey hairs You carry me!

128.

El Shaddai, the God of More Than Enough, I thank You that I have enough health to fulfill my full assignment!

(Genesis 17:1)

Praise be to God — I will not leave this earth early!

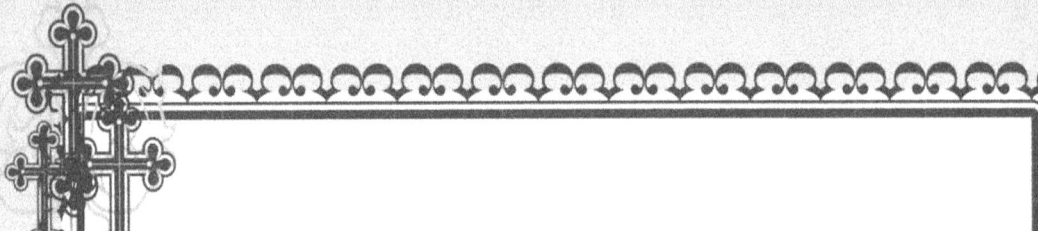

129.

Jesus, my Healing Covenant, I thank You that I walk daily in the fulfillment of divine health — no reversal!

(Deuteronomy 7:15)

Let fire protect my health contract!

130.

The God Who Keeps Me, I thank You that my organs will not fail, my mind will not forget, my body will not collapse!

(Psalm 121:7)

Hallelujah! Preservation is my portion!

131.

Ancient of Days, I adore You that my ending shall be greater than my beginning — glory shall crown my latter years!

(Job 42:12)

God I adore You — You beautify my future!

132.

Jesus, the Tree of Life, I thank You that I am planted in glory, and my fruit will not fail!

(Psalm 92:12–14)

Praise be to God — I will flourish till the end!

133.

El Roi, You see me and You chose me — I'm not too young, not too old, not too late to be healed!

(Genesis 16:13)

Let divine attention flood my timeline!

134.

Jehovah Tsidkenu, I thank You that righteousness has given me access to peace, healing, and longevity!

(Malachi 4:2)

Hallelujah! I rise with healing in Your wings!

135.

Jesus, the Lord of Times and Seasons, I thank You that no demonic calendar shall cut my life short!

(Ecclesiastes 3:1–2)

You are greater than the greatest — my times are in Your hands!

136.

The Glory of My Latter Days, I thank You that my final years will not be filled with pain but with power!

(Haggai 2:9)

Praise be to God — my ending will preach Your faithfulness!

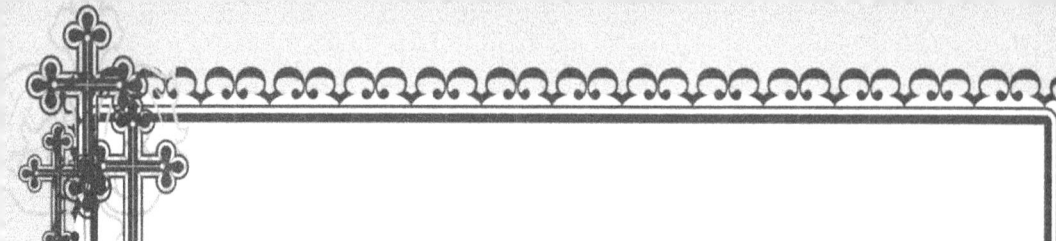

137.

The Giver of Breath, I thank You that every breath I take now glorifies You — not sickness, not fear!

(Isaiah 42:5)

God I adore You — breath by breath, I worship!

138.

Jesus, My Portion Forever, I thank You that no matter my age, You remain my strength and reward!

(Psalm 73:26)

Let my portion burn with eternal fire!

139.

The Everlasting Arm, I thank You for carrying me through every season — not one part of my life wasted!

(Deuteronomy 33:27)

Hallelujah! I am not abandoned in age!

140.

The Flame that Never Fades, I thank You that my fire won't go out in old age — it will intensify!

(Leviticus 6:13)

Let my grey hairs blaze with glory!

141.

Jesus, the Sustainer of My Soul, I thank You that even in old age I will bear fruit, stay fresh, and flourish in fire!

(Psalm 92:14)

Hallelujah! My latter years shall shine!

142.

El Olam, Everlasting God, I adore You that I am preserved by eternity, not broken by time!

(Isaiah 40:28–31)

God I adore You — Your strength outlives every weakness!

143.

The God Who Numbers My Days, I thank You that premature death is deleted from my scroll — long life is secured!

(Psalm 91:16)

Praise be to God! You are greater than statistics!

144.

Jesus, the Strength of My Life, I thank You that when I should be weak, I grow stronger — no decline, only rising!

(2 Corinthians 4:16)

Let the fire of youth rest upon me again!

145.

Jehovah Shammah, the Lord Who is There, I thank You that You will be with me in every decade — until the end and beyond!

(Matthew 28:20)

You are greater than the greatest — I am never alone!

146.

The King Eternal, I thank You that nothing can expire what You established in me — divine life has no expiry!

(1 Timothy 1:17)

Let eternal purpose erase temporary affliction!

147.

The Glory That Covers Me, I thank You that no shame, no scars, no symptoms remain — only fire, only glory!

(Isaiah 61:7)

Hallelujah! You clothed me in beauty and fire!

148.

Jesus, the Living One, I thank You that because You live, I shall live long and live well!

(John 14:19)

Praise be to God — You secured my future!

149.

The Flame of the Spirit, I thank You that my energy is renewed daily, not by food alone — but by fire!

(Romans 8:11)

Let Holy Ghost voltage charge my every cell!

150.

The Lifter of My Head, I adore You for restoring my posture, my joy, and my physical strength!

(Psalm 3:3)

God I adore You! I'm standing taller by Your glory!

151.

Jesus, My Perfect Example, I thank You that I shall finish strong, fulfill purpose, and exit this world in glory!

(2 Timothy 4:7–8)

No unfinished race — only completed fire!

152.

Jehovah Tsidkenu, I thank You that righteousness will extend my years and protect my legacy!

(Proverbs 10:27)

Hallelujah! My years are clothed in Your goodness!

153.

The Great Builder, I thank You that You've rebuilt my health brick by brick with heavenly materials!

(Nehemiah 2:18)

Praise be to God — no system left broken!

154.

Jesus, the Everlasting Light, I thank You that I will not walk into old age with darkness — only with revelation and rest!

(Isaiah 60:19)

Let Your light flood every remaining year!

155.

The Giver of Strength to the Weary, I thank You that supernatural stamina is my portion for the rest of my journey!

(Isaiah 40:29)

God I adore You — my strength will not fail!

156.

The Defender of the Righteous, I thank You for surrounding my final years with divine defense — no evil shall touch me!

(Psalm 34:7)

Let fire encamp around my days and nights!

157.

El Chaiyai, the God of My Life, I thank You for making every moment meaningful — no wasted days, no wasted breath!

(Psalm 42:8)

Hallelujah! My life is valuable and eternal!

158.

Jesus, the God of Restoration, I thank You that You've added back what sickness took — plus interest!

(Zechariah 9:12)

You are greater than the greatest!

159.

The Keeper of Israel, I thank You for watching over me day and night — I am safe until purpose is fulfilled!

(Psalm 121:4)

Praise be to God! I rest in total safety!

160.

The Righteous Judge, I thank You for ruling in my favor and declaring me fit for long life, fire, and fullness!

(Psalm 103:6)

Let Your gavel silence every false report!

161.

Jesus, the Ark of My Preservation, I thank You that while others may fall, I am carried safely into the future You wrote for me!

(Genesis 7:1; Psalm 91:7)

Hallelujah! I will not sink — I will rise!

162.

Jehovah-Gmolah, the God of recompense, I thank You for repaying me with joy, fire, and years of full restoration!

(Jeremiah 51:56)

You are greater than the greatest — what I lost, You have multiplied!

163.

The Light of My Path, I adore You for guiding me out of sickness into a destiny lined with fire, peace, and fruitfulness!

(Psalm 119:105)

God I adore You — I follow Your flame!

164.

El Elyon, the Most High God, I thank You that my years are governed by Heaven, not by genetics or statistics!

(Psalm 91:1; Lamentations 3:37)

Praise be to God — long life is my portion!

165.

Jesus, the Giver of Living Waters, I thank You for flushing every system in my body with divine vitality!

(John 4:14)

Let every dead thing rise by Your flow!

166.

The Lion of Judah, I thank You that one roar from You silenced every report, reversed every curse, and declared me whole!

(Revelation 5:5)

Hallelujah! The roar of healing never ends!

167.

Jehovah Mephalti, my Deliverer, I thank You for delivering me from every pit of pain, delay, and fear!

(Psalm 18:2)

God I adore You — You rescued me with fire!

168.

Jesus, the Door of Glory, I thank You for opening new seasons of health, strength, purpose, and supernatural energy!

(John 10:9)

Let this door never shut again — I walk in power!

169.

The Glory of Zion, I thank You for beautifying my days with wholeness, clarity, and unstoppable fire!

(Isaiah 60:1)

You are greater than the greatest — my life now radiates glory!

170.

The Flame That Guides, I thank You for not just healing me — but leading me into generational victory!

(Exodus 13:21)

Let fire guide my lineage forever!

171.

The Eternal Spirit, I thank You for renewing me daily — I will not rust, I will not decay, I will not collapse!

(2 Corinthians 4:16)

Praise be to God — I age in strength, not in weakness!

172.

Jesus, the Door of Escape, I thank You for creating escape routes from every trap of disease and destruction!

(1 Corinthians 10:13)

Let holy escape be my permanent route!

173.

Jehovah El Gemuwal, my Rewarder, I thank You for rewarding every cry, fast, prayer, and tear with glory!

(Hebrews 11:6)

Hallelujah! You saw it all — and paid in fire!

174.

The God of Seasons, I thank You for shifting me from a season of survival into a season of overflow and fire!

(Ecclesiastes 3:1)

God I adore You — my new season is here!

175.

Jesus, my Safe Place, I thank You that in every storm, I found shelter — and in that shelter, I found You!

(Psalm 91:1)

You are greater than the greatest — I survived because I abided!

176.

The God of Unfailing Promises, I thank You that Your Word concerning my healing cannot fail — it is sealed in Heaven!

(Numbers 23:19)

Praise be to God — what You said, You did!

177.

The High Tower, I thank You for elevating me above the reach of affliction — they may shoot, but I'm out of range!

(Proverbs 18:10)

Let fire protect my altitude!

178.

Jesus, the Strong Foundation, I thank You that my body is now stabilized on truth, not shaken by facts!

(Isaiah 28:16)

God I adore You — You are my medical final say!

179.

The God Who Turns Captivity, I thank You that my health testimony will be like a dream — sudden, complete, undeniable!

(Psalm 126:1–2)

Hallelujah! My mouth shall never be silent again!

180.

The Voice Over Many Waters, I thank You for speaking louder than every diagnosis — and Your Word carried power!

(Psalm 29:3–4)

You are greater than the greatest — I rise because You spoke!

181.

The Fire in My Bones, I thank You that no affliction can hide from Your flame — You burned it to the root!

(Jeremiah 20:9)

Hallelujah! My bones are now altars of fire!

182.

Jesus, my Waymaker, I thank You for opening the path of long life when every report said it was over!

(Isaiah 43:19)

Praise be to God — the door of destiny is wide open!

183.

Jehovah Shalom, I thank You for flooding my body with peace — no more torment, no more tension!

(Judges 6:24)

God I adore You — I now walk in fire and calm!

184.

The God of Completion, I thank You that no area of my healing is left unfinished — it is done, sealed, and established!

(Ecclesiastees 3:14)

Let glory crown the whole testimony!

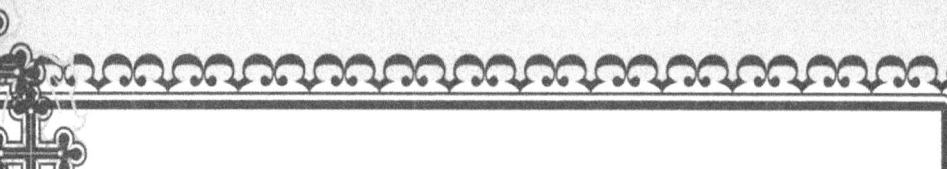

185.

The Breath of Life, I thank You that my lungs are full of praise, not pain — I inhale power and exhale testimony!

(Genesis 2:7)

Let every breath become revival!

186.

Jesus, my Defender, I thank You that You fought for me while I slept, wept, and waited — and You won!

(Exodus 14:14)

Hallelujah! My battles are now my breakthroughs!

187.

The God Who Breaks Chains, I thank You for shattering every chain of weakness, delay, depression, and defeat!

(Acts 12:7)

Praise be to God — I am out, I am free, I am fire!

188.

The Voice That Shakes the Earth, I thank You for speaking once — and every root of pain trembled and collapsed!

(Hebrews 12:26)

God I adore You — let everything shaken remain healed!

189.

Jesus, the Hope Restorer, I thank You for restoring my laughter, expectation, strength, and joy!

(Romans 15:13)

Let the river of hope flood every dry place!

190.

The Judge Who Overrules, I thank You that You canceled the death sentence and overruled every medical decree!

(Isaiah 54:17)

Hallelujah! I am living proof of divine justice!

191.

The God of Fire by Night, I thank You that even in my darkest season, You lit my path with mercy and miracles!

(Exodus 13:21)

Let every night turn to day under Your flame!

192.

Jesus, the One Who Was, Who Is, and Who Is to Come, I thank You that You healed my past, secured my now, and sealed my tomorrow!

(Revelation 1:8)

You are greater than time and stronger than affliction!

193.

The Glory That Fills the Temple, I thank You that my body is now filled with Your presence — sickness has no space!

(1 Corinthians 6:19)

God I adore You — fill this temple with holy fire!

194.

Jehovah Rohi, the Lord my Shepherd, I thank You for restoring my soul and guiding my steps back into divine health!

(Psalm 23:1–3)

Praise be to the One who led me into strength!

195.

The One Who Carries Me, I thank You for carrying me when I had no strength left — You became my legs, my lungs, my fight!

(Isaiah 46:4)

Let every moment I walk testify of You!

196.

Jesus, the Flame That Cannot Be Quenched, I thank You that no affliction, season, or devil can extinguish my fire!

(Leviticus 6:13)

Let my altar burn until eternity!

197.

The One Who Anoints My Head, I thank You for crowning me with divine health, mental clarity, and renewed youth!

(Psalm 23:5)

God I adore You — let my cup run over with strength!

198.

The Keeper of My Bones, I thank You that none shall be broken, infected, or wasted — You preserve me from within!

(Psalm 34:20)

Let divine preservation guard my skeleton!

199.

Jesus, My Reward, I thank You that fire, not fatigue, will accompany me into every new season!

(Hebrews 11:6)

Hallelujah! I don't limp into the future — I leap!

200.

Father, I thank You! You rewrote my life with fire. You restored my strength with power. You replaced fear with fire, weakness with worship, and sickness with supernatural victory.

I now walk in long life, radiant health, and divine preservation. Let every cell, every system, and every step shout: "The Lord has done this!"

Hallelujah! Let the glory remain, and the fire never die.

201.

Jesus, the Axe at the Root, I thank You for striking the foundation of affliction — no trace, no return, no delay!

(Matthew 3:10)

Hallelujah! Every root has been burned by fire!

202.

Jehovah Tsabaoth, Lord of Armies, I thank You that You've declared war on the systems behind my symptoms — and won!

(Psalm 46:7)

You are greater than the greatest — fire surrounds my body!

203.

El Elyon, the Most High, I thank You for raising me above the reach of reoccurring pain and generational infirmities!

(Psalm 91:1)

No power beneath can touch what You've lifted!

204.

The Ancient of Days, I thank You that ancient sicknesses bow to Your eternal decree!

(Daniel 7:9)

Praise be to God — ancient roots have been severed!

205.

The Consuming Fire, I adore You for burning every hidden seed of weakness before it could bear fruit again!

(Hebrews 12:29)

Let my body be untouchable by hidden darkness!

206.

Jesus, the Sword of Heaven, I thank You that Your Word has pierced to the root and silenced every source of affliction!

(Hebrews 4:12)

Let every evil plantation be cut down forever!

207.

Jehovah Mekoddishkem, my Sanctifier, I thank You for purging every defilement rooted in my bloodstream!

(Leviticus 20:8)

Hallelujah! My blood is clean, my life is holy!

208.

The Rock That Breaks in Pieces, I thank You for smashing generational patterns that tried to claim me!

(Jeremiah 23:29)

Let the cycle end permanently — no repeats, no residue!

209.

Jesus, the Root and Offspring of David, I thank You for uprooting the wrong and planting divine strength in me!

(Revelation 22:16)

What You plant, no devil can remove!

210.

El Qanna, the Jealous God, I thank You that no idol of sickness can dwell in a temple You've claimed with fire!

(Exodus 34:14)

This body belongs to God — no squatter shall remain!

211.

The Lord Who Sees, I thank You for identifying what no scan could detect and destroying it completely!

(Genesis 16:13)

Hallelujah! Nothing escapes the fire of Your eyes!

212.

Jesus, the Light of the World, I thank You for flooding every hidden corner of my being with truth and cleansing!

(John 8:12)

No shadow can survive the brightness of Your fire!

213.

The Refiner's Fire, I thank You for purifying my organs, my cells, and my blood like fine gold!

(Malachi 3:3)

Let the impurities melt under holy fire!

214.

The Lion of Judah, I thank You for roaring over my foundation and tearing apart every predator of my health!

(Amos 3:8)

Let the roar shake the root system of affliction!

215.

The Banner of My Victory, I thank You that under Your flag, no affliction can regroup or recover!

(Exodus 17:15)

Praise be to God — the battle is permanently won!

216.

Jesus, the Glory of My Body, I thank You that my bones, my tissues, and my systems now radiate with divine fire!

(Romans 8:11)

Let my body glow with glory, not weakness!

217.

The Breaker of Foundations, I thank You for destroying every inherited weakness I didn't even know I carried!

(Micah 2:13)

Let nothing ancient rise again in my bloodline!

218.

Jehovah Elohim, my Creator, I thank You that You're restoring me to factory settings — perfect, whole, complete!

(Genesis 1:26–27)

What You made, You've now rebuilt in glory!

219.

Jesus, the Carpenter of Nazareth, I thank You for rebuilding what affliction tried to dismantle — stronger than ever!

(Mark 6:3)

Let divine reconstruction overtake my life!

220.

The Fire That Cannot Be Quenched, I thank You that the fire You started in me will protect, preserve, and prevail!

(Leviticus 6:13)

God I adore You — this fire shall never go out!

221

Jesus, the Living Water, I thank You that Your flow has flushed out every hidden deposit of affliction!

(John 7:38)

Let Your stream purify my body from the root!

222.

The Ancient Deliverer, I thank You that ancient chains of sickness from my father's house are permanently broken!

(Nahum 1:13)

Hallelujah! No chain shall continue with me!

223.

El Channun, the Gracious God, I thank You that mercy located what medicine couldn't and reversed what man accepted!

(Psalm 145:8)

You are greater than the greatest! Glory!

224.

The Fire-Caller, I thank You that You called down fire on every altar where sickness was being reinforced!

(1 Kings 18:38)

Let holy fire consume the roots forever!

225.

Jesus, the Root Breaker, I thank You that generational sickness has no more say — the blood speaks better things!

(Hebrews 12:24)

God I adore You — You spoke, and the roots withered!

226.

The Builder of New Foundations, I thank You that You've established my body on strength, not struggle!

(Isaiah 28:16)

Let affliction never find a place to land again!

227.

The God Who Restores, I thank You for restoring years of strength that were stolen at the root!

(Joel 2:25)

Let divine repayment thunder across my timeline!

228.

Jesus, My Cleanser, I thank You for cleansing my systems of all hidden viruses, infections, and silent sabotage!

(1 John 1:9)

Let the blood flush out every hiding place of evil!

229.

The Guardian of My Temple, I thank You that You've shut every door sickness used to enter!

(Revelation 3:7)

Hallelujah! This temple is sealed in fire and glory!

230.

The One Who Makes All Things New, I thank You for giving me new blood, new breath, new bones — no damage remains!

(Revelation 21:5)

Let holy fire write a brand-new story in my flesh!

231.

Jehovah Rophe, my Healer, I thank You for healing what I didn't even know was broken — deeply, completely, permanently!

(Exodus 15:26)

Praise be to God! Nothing hidden shall remain!

232.

The Glory Cloud, I thank You that Your presence has moved into my life — and sickness has moved out forever!

(Exodus 40:34–38)

Let glory saturate every corner of my being!

233.

The Judge of All, I thank You for judging the roots of torment and casting down their altars forever!

(Isaiah 54:17)

Let affliction be declared illegal in my life!

234.

The Fire in My Foundation, I thank You that no inherited weakness shall survive this covenant fire!

(Isaiah 4:4)

God I adore You — Your fire is my new inheritance!

235.

The One Who Holds the Keys, I thank You that You've locked every backdoor of affliction and opened doors of power!

(Revelation 3:7)

Let divine security guard my life's future!

236.

Jesus, the Curse Crusher, I thank You that what afflicted generations now ends permanently with me!

(Galatians 3:13)

Hallelujah! My bloodline is rewritten by grace!

237.

The Repairer of Breaches, I thank You that what left gaps in my strength is now sealed with divine fire!

(Isaiah 58:12)

No room left for reentry — glory has filled the gaps!

238.

The One Who Upholds Me, I thank You that even when I faltered, You didn't let sickness overtake me!

(Isaiah 41:10)

You are greater than the greatest — You held me in mercy!

239.

The One Who Commands Wholeness, I thank You for commanding strength to rise, healing to manifest, and roots to die!

(Mark 11:21)

Let every cursed root remain dry forever!

240.

The Final Say, I thank You that what You declared cannot be challenged — healing is mine, and affliction has lost!

(Lamentations 3:37)

Praise be to God! You said it — and it is so!

241.

Jesus, my Strong Tower, I thank You that no weapon formed against my body shall prosper — not then, not now, not ever!

(Isaiah 54:17)

Hallelujah! You are my divine firewall!

242.

The God of Unapproachable Light, I thank You that darkness cannot trace or touch me — I live in divine brightness!

(1 Timothy 6:16)

Let every shadow be scattered forever!

243.

Jehovah Gmolah, the God of recompense, I thank You for paying back the devil with interest — for every hour he tried to steal!

(Isaiah 61:7)

You are greater than the greatest — I recover all!

244.

Jesus, the Stone the Builders Rejected, I thank You for becoming the unshakable foundation of my healing!

(Psalm 118:22)

The devil is under my feet — crushed permanently!

245.

The God of Elijah, I thank You for sending down fire to burn the ropes of sickness and shame from my life!

(1 Kings 18:38)

Let the fire fall and expose every false altar!

246.

The Man of War, I thank You that You entered my battle and fought until I emerged victorious!

(Exodus 15:3)

Praise be to God — the devil is defeated for life!

247.

Jesus, the Deliverer of Zion, I thank You for casting out every evil hand assigned to delay my recovery!

(Obadiah 1:17)

Hallelujah! I walk in fire-cleansed dominion!

248.

The One Who Rides the Heavens, I thank You that You rode over every storm to bring healing to my door!

(Deuteronomy 33:26)

The devil was disarmed mid-flight! Glory!

249.

The Consuming Fire, I thank You that every weapon, word, and witchcraft is burned without mercy!

(Hebrews 12:29)

Let every spiritual cancer turn to smoke!

250.

The Lamb Who Was Slain, I thank You that the blood speaks louder than pain, reports, and fear!

(Revelation 12:11)

God I adore You — the blood has won!

251.

The Lord of Hosts, I thank You that angels war while I worship — my healing is divinely enforced!

(Psalm 103:20–21)

Let my praise stir up more angels!

252.

The Breaker of Oppression, I thank You for snapping every demonic assignment written in hell against me!

(Isaiah 10:27)

Let yokes break permanently in Jesus' name!

253.

Jesus, the Hammer of Heaven, I thank You for smashing every idol of sickness built over my life or family!

(Jeremiah 23:29)

Let the hammer strike until no altar remains!

254.

The Fire That Surrounds, I thank You for encircling my mind, organs, and days with undying flame!

(Zechariah 2:5)

The enemy shall see fire and flee in shame!

255.

The One Who Spoke and It Was, I thank You that one word from You shattered every medical verdict!

(Psalm 33:9)

Let Your Word keep echoing in my bloodstream!

256.

The Lord Strong and Mighty, I thank You for standing between me and destruction — You stood and I lived!

(Psalm 24:8)

Hallelujah! I now walk in divine recovery!

257.

The Fire Baptizer, I thank You for baptizing my body with holy flames — sickness has no space to return!

(Luke 3:16)

Let the flame stay permanent — eternal immunity!

258.

Jesus, the Lion and the Lamb, I thank You for bleeding for me and roaring for me — the devil didn't expect that!

(Revelation 5:5–6)

You are greater than the greatest — my Defender and Healer!

259.

The One Who Numbers My Tears, I thank You for turning every tear into a testimony of thunder and healing!

(Psalm 56:8)

Let my story silence satan's schemes forever!

260.

The King of Kings, I thank You that no diagnosis can rule where You reign — Your crown crushes every curse!

(Revelation 19:16)

Praise be to God — the King has spoken!

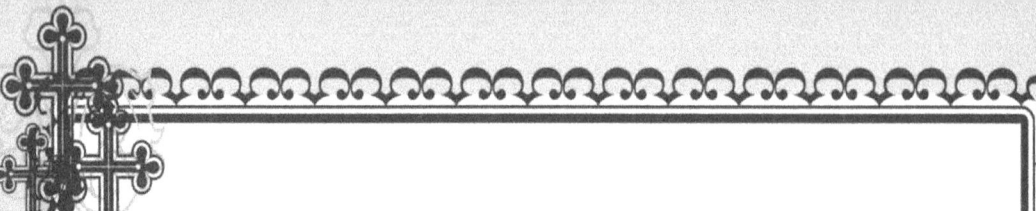

261.

Jesus, the Final Word, I thank You that the devil's sentence was overruled by Your blood and buried in fire!

(Lamentations 3:37)

Hallelujah! What You say, stands forever!

262.

The Shield Around Me, I thank You that sickness bounces off the covenant covering You placed upon my life!

(Psalm 3:3)

Let no arrow find access again — fire is my shield!

263.

Jehovah El-Nose, the God Who Lifts, I thank You for lifting me out of affliction and crowning me with restoration!

(Psalm 30:1)

God I adore You — You lifted me and left the devil speechless!

264.

The Fire From Your Throne, I thank You for judging the strongman assigned to monitor my health!

(Revelation 4:5)

Let every throne of darkness be thrown down!

265.

Jesus, My Stronghold, I thank You that I am too hidden in Your glory for the devil to find or touch again!

(Psalm 27:5)

Praise be to God — I am sealed in a fortress of fire!

266.

The God Who Restores My Soul, I thank You for healing not just my body but the weariness of warfare!

(Psalm 23:3)

Let refreshing flood every chamber of my heart!

267.

El Chaiyai, the God of My Life, I thank You that I live because of You — not by man's report, not by circumstance!

(Psalm 42:8)

Hallelujah! I am carried by divine breath!

268.

The One Who Breaks Gates, I thank You for smashing demonic gates of sickness erected in the spirit!

(Isaiah 45:2)

Let the iron bars melt in the presence of glory!

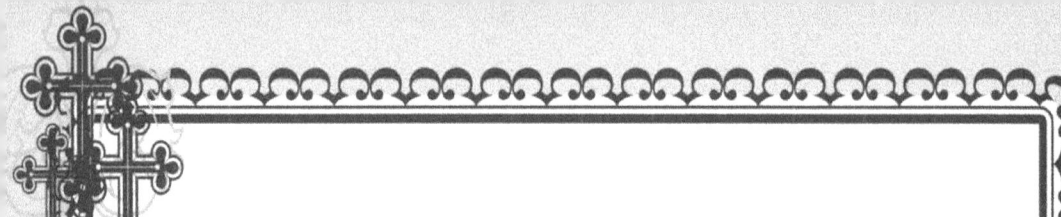

269.

Jesus, My Rescue Story, I thank You that my healing is not quiet — it's loud, public, and undeniable!

(Psalm 126:1–3)

You are greater than the greatest — You rescued me with fire!

270.

The Finger of God, I thank You for pointing at every hidden trap and turning it into a testimony!

(Luke 11:20)

Let divine precision destroy every trap of sickness!

271.

The Alpha and the Omega, I thank You for beginning my healing and sealing the ending with power and permanence!

(Revelation 22:13)

God I adore You — I lack nothing, I finish strong!

272.

The Lord Who Sanctifies, I thank You that You made me too holy to host affliction — fire lives here now!

(Leviticus 20:8)

Let my body be consecrated by flame and praise!

273.

The Commander of the Wind, I thank You for sweeping away every residue of pain with a blast from Heaven!

(Exodus 14:21)

Let fresh wind blow through every room of my body!

274.

Jesus, the Chain Breaker, I thank You that no monitoring spirit can track what You've broken and buried!

(Acts 12:7)

Let the chains fall and never be found again!

275.

The One Who Touched the Leper, I thank You that You still touch what others call untouchable — and turn shame into healing!

(Mark 1:40–42)

Hallelujah! Nothing is too far gone for You!

276.

The Guardian of My Gateways, I thank You for sealing every spiritual portal that once let affliction in!

(Psalm 121:8)

Let glory lock every gate — permanently!

277.

The Fire That Speaks, I thank You that Your glory is louder than symptoms — and Your Word burns away every lie!

(Jeremiah 5:14)

Let every report bow to Your flaming truth!

278.

Jesus, the Name Above Every Name, I thank You that no disease, condition, or pain can stand in Your presence!

(Philippians 2:9–10)

Praise be to God — sickness bows and flees!

279.

The Lord Who Opens, I thank You that You opened doors of healing that the devil swore I'd never enter!

(Isaiah 22:22)

Let the door of wholeness never shut again!

280.

The Thunder That Shakes Hell, I thank You that Your voice disrupted every meeting where my name was mentioned in darkness!

(Psalm 29:3–9)

Let every demonic discussion catch fire!

281.

The Covering of My Head, I thank You for silencing mental attacks and crowning me with peace and power!

(Psalm 140:7)

Let my thoughts be guarded with holy fire!

282.

Jesus, My Banner, I thank You that I fly the flag of victory — and the enemy now salutes my healing!

(Exodus 17:15)

God I adore You — Your banner is upon me forever!

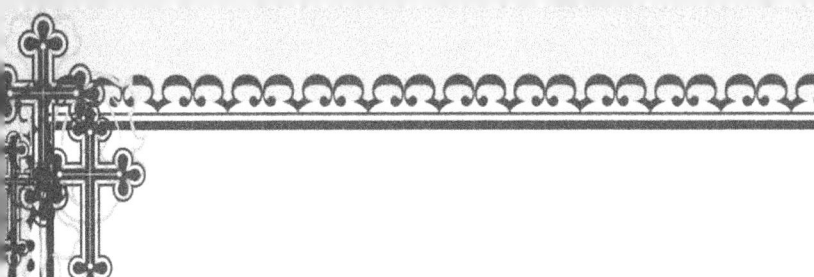

283.

The Giver of Victory, I thank You that even in my weakest moment, You fought — and I won!

(2 Corinthians 2:14)

Let my life shout: The Lord has done this!

284.

Jehovah Go'el, my Redeemer, I thank You for redeeming my health, my timeline, and my testimony!

(Isaiah 43:1)

Praise be to God — the fire of redemption still burns!

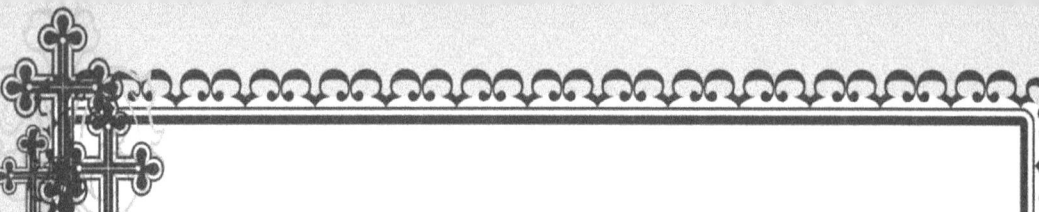

285.

The Lamb on the Throne, I thank You that mercy triumphed over judgment — and glory was poured out like oil!

(Revelation 5:6)

Hallelujah! The throne ruled in my favor!

286.

Jesus, the Master of Breakthroughs, I thank You that no satanic blockade could stop the flow of my healing!

(2 Samuel 5:20)

Let every wall break like water before my God!

287.

The Commander of Glory, I thank You for commanding light into the darkness of disease — and commanding it to flee!

(2 Corinthians 4:6)

Let the voice of fire echo in my blood!

288.

The Lion of Judah, I thank You for devouring every serpent of affliction that dared to enter my territory!

(Psalm 91:13)

God I adore You — the roar has silenced the hiss!

289.

Jehovah Jireh, my Provider, I thank You for providing divine immunity, supernatural strength, and overflow!

(Genesis 22:14)

You are greater than the greatest — I lack nothing!

290.

The Flame of the Altar, I thank You that every sacrifice of praise has released fire to consume my enemies!

(Leviticus 9:24)

Let thanksgiving trigger judgment on sickness!

291.

The Storm Stopper, I thank You for rebuking storms of pain and fear with one word — Peace!

(Mark 4:39)

Praise be to God — my calm is fire-filled!

292.

Jesus, the Resurrection Voice, I thank You that what others buried in grief, You raised in glory!

(John 11:43–44)

Let my body walk out of every grave with joy!

293.

El Shaddai, the All-Sufficient One, I thank You that no deficiency can live in me — I am full, whole, and restored!

(Genesis 17:1)

Hallelujah! You overflow every empty space!

294.

The Fire That Fills the Temple, I thank You that my body now radiates Your glory — not one room is empty!

(2 Chronicles 7:1)

Let divine smoke dwell in my bones!

295.

Jesus, the Voice Above Waters, I thank You for speaking above every lie, every fear, and every false report!

(Psalm 29:3–4)

God I adore You — Your thunder restores me!

296.

The Sword of the Spirit, I thank You for dividing truth from deception and cutting out every root of inherited torment!

(Hebrews 4:12)

Let Your sword leave no sickness untouched!

297.

The One Who Wipes Every Tear, I thank You for turning weeping nights into dancing mornings!

(Psalm 30:5)

Praise be to God — laughter is now my medicine!

298.

The God of Wonders, I thank You that my recovery shall be called miraculous — undeniable, unexplainable, divine!

(Psalm 77:14)

Let my life become a billboard of healing glory!

299.

Jesus, my Stronghold, I thank You that while others fainted, You held me up and set me apart for fire-wrapped health!

(Psalm 18:2)

You are greater than the greatest — I'm fire-kept!

300.

Father, I thank You! The war is over. The devil is defeated. The roots are burned. The body is healed. The gates are sealed. The glory remains.

I walk in divine healing, long life, and supernatural praise. This testimony is permanent, powerful, and prophetic.

Hallelujah! What You have done — no power can undo. Let this fire speak for generations!

301.

Jesus, the Root of David, I thank You that every evil root has dried up — only holy fire remains in my foundation!

(Revelation 22:16)

Let divine roots replace every wicked seed!

302.

The God Who Answers by Fire, I thank You that Your answer overpowered every demonic question over my health!

(1 Kings 18:24)

Hallelujah! The fire answered and hell retreated!

303.

The God of No Limits, I thank You for exceeding the timeline, the symptoms, and the expectations — You did more!

(Ephesians 3:20)

Praise be to God — I received beyond request!

304.

Jesus, the King of Glory, I thank You that You lifted the gates, destroyed the bars, and entered with healing!

(Psalm 24:7–10)

Let healing glory flood every system!

305.

The One Who Sits Above the Circle of the Earth, I thank You that Your dominion over my life is irreversible!

(Isaiah 40:22)

No affliction can rise above Your throne!

306.

The Burning Bush God, I thank You that I burn with Your fire — but I am not consumed!

(Exodus 3:2)

Let divine flame protect and preserve me daily!

307.

The Commander of Heaven's Armies, I thank You for assigning angels to destroy every affliction behind the scenes!

(Psalm 91:11; 2 Kings 6:17)

Let angelic fire patrol my entire being!

308.

Jesus, the Son of Righteousness, I thank You that Your wings brought healing, and Your light blinded every enemy!

(Malachi 4:2)

Hallelujah! I rise under healing glory!

309.

Jehovah Rohi, my Shepherd, I thank You for leading me out of confusion and into covenant wholeness!

(Psalm 23:1–3)

God I adore You — I shall not want for health again!

310.

The Defender of the Innocent, I thank You for stepping in when I had no strength left to pray — You carried me!

(Psalm 10:17–18)

Praise be to God — mercy fought while I slept!

311.

Jesus, my Sure Foundation, I thank You that no flood, no fire, and no fact can shake the healing You built in me!

(Isaiah 28:16)

Let my strength be unmovable in glory!

312.

The Alpha of My Healing, I thank You that what You started in fire, You will finish with glory!

(Philippians 1:6)

Let healing mature into unstoppable testimony!

313.

The Great Refiner, I thank You that affliction refined me, but fire preserved me — and now, I shine!

(Malachi 3:3)

Let the gold of my healing testify of You!

314.

The Flame Upon My Altar, I thank You that my thanksgiving has turned into a furnace of permanent restoration!

(Leviticus 6:13)

Let the altar burn and never go out!

315.

The Giver of Good Gifts, I thank You for giving me strength with no sorrow, peace with no pain, life with no limit!

(James 1:17)

You are greater than the greatest — You gave it all!

316.

Jesus, My Rescue Commander, I thank You for launching divine raids against every spirit that tormented my health!

(Psalm 18:16–19)

Let fire surround me like a military base!

317.

The One Who Calls Me by Name, I thank You that affliction cannot rename what You've already called "healed!"

(Isaiah 43:1)

Let Heaven's name override the enemy's label!

318.

The Thunder of God, I thank You for shaking every demonic surveillance into silence and scattering their plans!

(Psalm 29:3–9)

Let divine thunder paralyze my adversaries!

319.

The Breath in My Lungs, I thank You that every breath is a weapon, every exhale is praise, and every inhale is power!

(Genesis 2:7)

God I adore You — I breathe the atmosphere of glory!

320.

The Owner of My Body, I thank You that the devil lost the lease and You took full possession of Your temple!

(1 Corinthians 6:19–20)

Let Your glory remain and reign in this house!

321.

The God of Justice, I thank You for judging every wicked root of long-standing affliction in my life!

(Psalm 103:6)

Hallelujah! Let justice roll like fire through my bloodline!

322.

Jesus, the Chain-Breaker, I thank You for breaking cycles of sickness that trapped generations before me!

(Isaiah 10:27)

God I adore You — I am the curse-breaker in my family!

323.

The Voice of Many Waters, I thank You for drowning every demonic whisper that tried to speak again in my body!

(Revelation 1:15)

Let every voice of darkness be silenced by thunder!

324.

The King of Healing, I thank You that no throne of disease can reign in my body — only You are enthroned here!

(Psalm 22:3)

Praise be to God — my temple belongs to the King!

325.

The Root and Offspring of David, I thank You for uprooting evil patterns and planting divine fire instead!

(Revelation 22:16)

Let only glory grow in this soil!

326.

Jehovah Gibbor Milchamah, the Lord Mighty in Battle, I thank You for fighting behind the scenes and securing my restoration!

(Psalm 24:8)

Let the gates of affliction lift and flee in Your presence!

327.

Jesus, the Door No Man Can Shut, I thank You for locking sickness out and sealing me into divine immunity!

(Revelation 3:8)

Hallelujah! The gate of healing is forever open!

328.

The Fire That Defends, I thank You for shielding me from every second wave of attack — retaliation is forbidden!

(Isaiah 4:5–6)

Let fire be my firewall — day and night!

329.

The One Who Keeps My Foot From Slipping, I thank You for keeping me from falling back into patterns of defeat!

(Psalm 121:3)

God I adore You — You upheld me when I staggered!

330.

The Builder and Restorer, I thank You that what was damaged has now become the foundation of glory!

(Isaiah 61:4)

Let glory rise from what the enemy tried to break!

331.

Jesus, the Prince of Peace, I thank You that peace now rules my blood pressure, my heartbeat, my hormones, and my breath!

(John 14:27)

Let peace become my permanent rhythm!

332.

The Living Word, I thank You that You spoke and the sentence of death reversed instantly!

(Psalm 107:20)

Let every word You sent complete its assignment in my body!

333.

The Great High Priest, I thank You for interceding over me even when I had no words left — You prayed me into healing!

(Hebrews 7:25)

You are greater than the greatest — You stood in my gap!

334.

The One Who Calls the Things That Be Not, I thank You for calling me healed while I was still bleeding!

(Romans 4:17)

Let Your words override every human observation!

335.

The Light That Cannot Be Hidden, I thank You that Your healing has become visible, undeniable, and unshakable in my life!

(Matthew 5:14–16)

Let my story light up the nations with praise!

336.

Jesus, the Flame in My Spirit, I thank You for setting my soul ablaze — every trace of weakness has been consumed!

(Luke 24:32)

Let holy fire fuel my future!

337.

The Master of Times and Seasons, I thank You for ending the season of struggle and launching the era of glory!

(Ecclesiastes 3:1)

Let fire mark the change of times forever!

338.

The God Who Sees in Secret, I thank You for healing me in places only You could see!

(Matthew 6:6)

God I adore You — You healed the parts I couldn't explain!

339.

The Giver of Long Life, I thank You that my days shall be many, fruitful, fire-filled, and fulfilled!

(Psalm 91:16)

Praise be to God — I shall not be cut short!

340.

Jesus, My Testimony, I thank You that the devil lost, sickness failed, and Heaven wrote my name in the victory column!

(Revelation 12:11)

Let this testimony be sealed forever in glory!

341.

Jesus, my Risen King, I thank You that because You rose, I rise daily — above affliction, above fear, above death!

(Romans 6:9)

Hallelujah! The grave has lost its voice!

342.

The Commander of Wholeness, I thank You for commanding every system in my body to come into divine alignment!

(Mark 5:41)

Let divine order stand forever!

343.

El Shaddai, God Almighty, I thank You that there's no weakness too strong for You to overpower — You are enough!

(Genesis 17:1)

Praise be to God — I'm healed by sufficiency!

344.

The God of Thunder, I thank You for sending a shockwave through the camp of the enemy — their weapons melted like wax!

(Psalm 29:3–5)

Let thunder announce my total recovery!

345.

The One Who Breathes on Bones, I thank You for breathing life into every dry system — I am standing, walking, and praising!

(Ezekiel 37:10)

God I adore You — what was dead is now dancing!

346.

The Restorer of Dignity, I thank You that shame and dependency are behind me — I rise clothed in strength!

(Isaiah 61:7)

Let royalty replace the garments of pain!

347.

Jesus, my Living Hope, I thank You that despair has been evicted — and hope has set up a throne in my chest!

(Romans 15:13)

Let my heart become a cathedral of praise!

348.

The One Who Rides on the Clouds, I thank You for riding over storms to land healing in my life!

(Psalm 104:3)

You are greater than the greatest — and You remembered me!

349.

Jehovah Tsur, my Rock, I thank You that I no longer wobble — my healing is solid, stable, and sealed!

(Psalm 18:2)

Let every step be unshakable in strength!

350.

The Voice in the Fire, I thank You that You spoke to me through the furnace and changed my identity forever!

(Exodus 3:4)

Let fire carry my name in the spirit realm!

351.

Jesus, the Firstborn from the Dead, I thank You for making me a firstfruit of freedom and recovery in my family!

(Colossians 1:18)

Let my testimony break generational limits!

352.

The One Who Turns Ashes into Beauty, I thank You that I now shine where I once wept!

(Isaiah 61:3)

Let every scar become a star!

353.

The God Who Lifts the Poor from the Dust, I thank You for lifting me from affliction and seating me in fire-clothed honor!

(1 Samuel 2:8)

Let my elevation mock the enemy's effort!

354.

The Caller of Stars by Name, I thank You that You called my name when affliction tried to silence it forever!

(Isaiah 40:26)

Hallelujah! Let my voice be fire in the earth!

355.

The Everlasting Father, I thank You for fathering my healing — You nurtured me until fire bloomed from my bones!

(Isaiah 9:6)

Let the tenderness of glory guard me forever!

356.

The One Who Anoints My Head with Oil, I thank You for crowning me with strength that sickness cannot wear out!

(Psalm 23:5)

Let my cup overflow with glory, not fear!

357.

Jesus, my Banner and Shield, I thank You that no fiery dart could land — You caught every one with fire!

(Ephesians 6:16)

Let the battlefield testify — I am untouchable!

358.

The King of the Ages, I thank You for teaching me that divine timing is better than medical timelines!

(Ecclesiastes 3:11)

Let Your timing continue to birth my miracles!

359.

The One Who Rides the Heavens, I thank You for delivering healing like lightning — fast, fierce, and final!

(Deuteronomy 33:26)

Let acceleration be the new normal in my body!

360.

The One Who Trains My Hands for War, I thank You for training my mouth to fire thanksgiving and my praise to crush devils!

(Psalm 144:1)

Let every word I speak become a fire missile!

361.

Jesus, the Ancient Breaker, I thank You that no disease — no matter how old — can survive Your eternal fire!

(Nahum 1:9)

Hallelujah! You broke the ancient yoke forever!

362.

The Name Above Every Name, I thank You that no diagnosis is higher than Your Name — cancer, diabetes, paralysis, all must bow!

(Philippians 2:9–11)

You are greater than the greatest — sickness bows!

363.

The Healer of the Incurable, I thank You for healing what experts called impossible — You reversed it by fire!

(Jeremiah 30:17)

God I adore You — the incurable has become the testimony!

364.

The One Who Carries My Sorrows, I thank You that pain has been laid on You, and I no longer carry what You conquered!

(Isaiah 53:4)

Let the burden remain buried at Calvary!

365.

The Fire in My Blood, I thank You that every infection, virus, inflammation, and imbalance has been incinerated!

(Malachi 4:2)

Let Your wings of healing sweep through my bloodstream!

366.

The One Who Restores What Was Lost, I thank You for restoring mobility, memory, energy, and everything sickness stole!

(Joel 2:25)

Let divine compensation flood my life!

367.

The God Who Turns Things Around, I thank You for turning prolonged sickness into permanent celebration!

(Psalm 30:11)

Let dancing echo louder than diagnosis!

368.

The One Who Does Not Forget, I thank You for remembering every prayer, every groan, every tear — and answering with power!

(Malachi 3:16)

Praise be to God — the fire heard me!

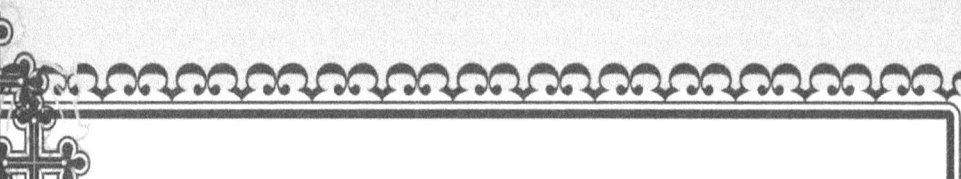

369.

Jesus, my Evidence, I thank You that I'm no longer just a believer — I'm proof that healing still happens!

(Psalm 103:2–3)

Let my life preach louder than any preacher!

370.

The Same Yesterday, Today, and Forever, I thank You that what You did in the Bible, You've done for me — and more!

(Hebrews 13:8)

You are greater than the timeline of sickness!

371.

The Judge Who Overrules, I thank You that chronic disease has no final say — Heaven's gavel has dropped in my favor!

(Lamentations 3:37)

Let every evil report be reversed by fire!

372.

The One Who Answers Suddenly, I thank You for sudden healing, sudden strength, sudden restoration — fire without warning!

(Isaiah 48:3)

Let speed become my new testimony!

373.

The God Who Keeps Covenant, I thank You that You never break Your Word — healing is not a maybe, it's a promise!

(Psalm 89:34)

Hallelujah! Your oath is sealed in glory!

374.

The Breaker of Every Chain, I thank You that emotional affliction, trauma, and torment have been cast into holy fire!

(Isaiah 61:1)

God I adore You — my soul is finally free!

375.

The Fire That Finds What's Hidden, I thank You for locating every disease hidden from scans, bloodwork, and experts — and destroying it!

(Hebrews 4:13)

Let no secret sickness survive Your flame!

376.

Jesus, my Great Physician, I thank You that You didn't just prescribe — You performed supernatural surgery and I walked out whole!

(Mark 2:17)

Let divine results silence natural records!

377.

The One Who Gives Double, I thank You for restoring double strength for every year the devil tried to take!

(Isaiah 61:7)

Let divine replacement double my fire!

378.

The Terror of Darkness, I thank You that every demonic power assigned to monitor my health has been scattered by thunder!

(Psalm 18:14)

Let the camp of the wicked remain in confusion!

379.

The Shield of My Days, I thank You for defending me from delayed healing, spiritual sabotage, and subtle sickness!

(Psalm 5:12)

Let the armor of praise remain on me forever!

380.

The God Who Hears Even Silence, I thank You for healing me even when I had no words — my groans became fire on Your altar!

(Romans 8:26)

You are greater than the greatest — You heard me and healed me!

381.

Jesus, the Resurrection and the Life, I thank You for raising me from affliction's grip — I'm no longer the patient, I'm the proof!

(John 11:25)

Hallelujah! My healing is not theory — it's testimony!

382.

Jehovah Shalom, I thank You for replacing torment with peace, anxiety with calm, and confusion with clarity!

(Judges 6:24)

Praise be to God — my peace now terrifies the enemy!

383.

The King Who Restores, I thank You that You restored what the enemy swore I'd never get back — time, joy, strength, and fire!

(Joel 2:25)

Let my restoration humiliate the kingdom of darkness!

384.

The Author of Life, I thank You that sickness cannot edit the script You wrote — I live, I rise, I reign!

(Acts 3:15)

God I adore You — You wrote the ending in fire!

385.

The One Who Stopped the Bleeding, I thank You that the flow of affliction has dried up forever — virtue has made me whole!

(Mark 5:29–34)

Let fire seal what faith unlocked!

386.

The Fountain That Never Runs Dry, I thank You that Your power continues to flood me with strength daily!

(Psalm 36:9)

Let divine refreshment never cease in my bones!

387.

The God of the Suddenly, I thank You that what delayed for years was reversed in a moment — instantly, undeniably, eternally!

(Acts 2:2)

Hallelujah! Sudden fire reversed slow death!

388.

The One Who Walked Through Walls, I thank You that no barrier stopped You from reaching the broken places in me!

(John 20:19)

You are greater than any defense hell tried to build!

389.

Jesus, my Anchor in the Storm, I thank You that I didn't drown — I discovered new depths of fire and favor!

(Hebrews 6:19)

Praise be to God — the storm strengthened me!

390.

The One Who Calls the Dead to Life, I thank You for calling vitality back into places doctors abandoned!

(Romans 4:17)

Let life burst through the grave of every cell!

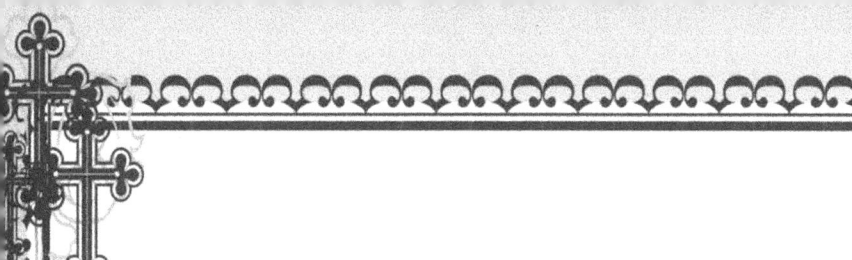

391.

Jehovah Immeka, the God Who Is With Me, I thank You for never leaving me in the battle — You fought beside me and in me!

(Psalm 46:1)

Let Emmanuel be praised forever!

392.

The One Who Holds the Keys, I thank You for locking affliction out of my future — and unlocking divine overflow!

(Revelation 3:7)

Let every gate You opened remain open forever!

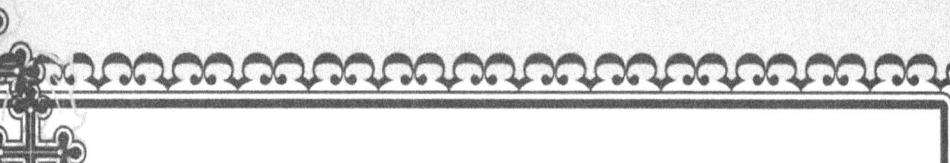

393.

Jesus, the Revealer of Secrets, I thank You for uncovering the spiritual roots of physical attacks and burning them down!

(Daniel 2:22)

Let every hidden affliction stay exposed and destroyed!

394.

The Commander of Light, I thank You for flooding my inner world with revelation and chasing out every shadow of fear!

(Psalm 119:130)

Let divine light reign where darkness once claimed!

395.

The God of Overflow, I thank You that I'm not just healed — I'm overflowing in energy, vision, and purpose!

(John 10:10)

Let abundance replace affliction forever!

396.

Jesus, the Man of Sorrows, I thank You that You bore every pain — I refuse to carry what You already crushed!

(Isaiah 53:4–5)

Hallelujah! The Cross ended the case!

397.

The Lord Who Satisfies Me Early, I thank You that I don't have to wait until later — healing is now, peace is now, fire is now!

(Psalm 90:14)

Let early satisfaction shame late affliction!

398.

The Giver of Glory, I thank You for clothing me in splendor where I once wore hospital gowns and sorrow!

(Psalm 3:3)

Let every memory of weakness turn into fireproof worship!

399.

The Owner of My Destiny, I thank You for reclaiming what sickness tried to cancel — I will finish my race with fire!

(2 Timothy 4:7–8)

You are greater than the greatest — my story ends in glory!

400.

Father, I thank You! The devil has been disgraced, sickness has been disarmed, and my body has become Your temple of fire.

Every root is destroyed. Every trace is erased. Every breath I take announces, "The Lord has done this!"

Let thanksgiving cover me like armor. Let glory clothe me like fire. And let healing rise in me like the dawn.

Hallelujah! Praise be to God! I am free. I am whole. I am fire-sealed — forever!

401.

Jesus, the Door of Life, I thank You for opening gates of wholeness that no affliction can shut!

(John 10:9)

Hallelujah! I walk in and never return to affliction again!

402.

The Rock That Cannot Be Moved, I thank You that no wave of relapse, fear, or lies can shake the healing You've established!

(Psalm 62:2)

Let divine stability reign in my body!

403.

Jehovah Mekoddishkem, the God Who Makes Me Holy, I thank You that my body is now too sanctified to host disease!

(Leviticus 20:8)

God I adore You — You've made me holy and whole!

404.

Jesus, my Healer and King, I thank You that Your rule has ended every torment that once ruled over me!

(Matthew 4:23)

Let Your Kingdom reign from head to toe!

405.

The One Who Wipes the Slate Clean, I thank You that You've erased every medical history, and written glory instead!

(Colossians 2:14)

Let every former report be swallowed in fire!

406.

The God Who Reverses the Irreversible, I thank You that conditions called "chronic" have been burned to nothing!

(Luke 1:37)

You are greater than the greatest — and greater than science!

407.

The Fire That Keeps Burning, I thank You that this flame of restoration shall never die out in me!

(Leviticus 6:13)

Praise be to God — let my altar stay hot forever!

408.

Jesus, the Resurrection at Work in Me, I thank You that even what was lost long ago has now been restored with fire!

(John 11:25)

Let resurrection fire restore everything!

409.

The One Who Binds Up the Broken, I thank You for healing not just symptoms — but my soul, mind, and history!

(Psalm 147:3)

Hallelujah! Wholeness has visited every dimension of me!

410.

The Lion of Judah, I thank You for roaring over every hidden root of infirmity — and silencing the serpent forever!

(Amos 3:8)

Let the roar echo through generations!

411.

The One Who Rewrites Stories, I thank You that what began in pain is ending in power — and what began in fire ends in glory!

(Genesis 50:20)

You are greater than the greatest — You changed my name and my record!

412.

The God of the Unexpected, I thank You for healing me in ways I never imagined, and faster than I thought!

(Isaiah 48:3)

Let surprises of glory fill my life forever!

413.

Jesus, the Great High Priest, I thank You for carrying my case into Heaven's courtroom and winning it by blood!

(Hebrews 4:14)

Let the verdict be fire: Healed! Restored! Preserved!

414.

The One Who Pours Oil and Wine, I thank You for pouring divine therapy into every wound, seen and unseen!

(Luke 10:34)

Let holy oil flood my marrow, my memories, and my blood!

415.

The God Who Delivers Without Scars, I thank You that I've come out of this fire without smoke, without smell, without stain!

(Daniel 3:27)

Praise be to God — I am proof of perfect preservation!

416.

The Warrior With Flaming Eyes, I thank You that Your gaze melted every evil eye that looked against my health!

(Revelation 1:14)

Let the fire in Your eyes scatter darkness forever!

417.

The Lord Who Covers Me, I thank You that Your wings shielded me from attacks I didn't even see!

(Psalm 91:4)

Let the feathers of fire wrap me forever!

418.

Jesus, the Great Interrupter, I thank You that You interrupted the timeline of affliction and started a new era of glory!

(Luke 7:14–15)

Let every delay be cut short by divine intervention!

419.

The Giver of Perfect Gifts, I thank You that healing is not borrowed — it is a gift from Your glory!

(James 1:17)

Let this gift never be returned or stolen!

420.

The King of Heaven's Armies, I thank You that my body is now guarded by angels, watched by glory, and sealed by fire!

(Psalm 34:7)

Hallelujah! Every gate is now divine property!

421.

Jesus, my Final Authority, I thank You that Your Word canceled the enemy's diagnosis and sealed my testimony with fire!

(Lamentations 3:37)

Let every satanic opinion be overruled forever!

422.

The Lord of the Harvest, I thank You that my season of sowing in tears has reaped healing, glory, and joy!

(Psalm 126:5)

Praise be to God — I now harvest in fire!

423.

The Living Flame, I thank You for keeping my altar burning when I had no strength left to fight!

(Leviticus 6:13)

Let the fire of praise never go out!

424.

The Breaker of the Gate, I thank You that You shattered the prison doors of prolonged affliction and led me out singing!

(Micah 2:13)

Hallelujah! My exit was written in fire!

425.

The King Who Comes Through Walls, I thank You for reaching the rooms in my body that doctors could never touch!

(John 20:19)

Let Your glory enter every sealed place!

426.

The Repairer of Breaches, I thank You that You restored what sickness tried to ruin — and rebuilt it in glory!

(Isaiah 58:12)

God I adore You — no gaps remain in my health!

427.

Jesus, the Light in My Darkness, I thank You that You ended the night of suffering with one word: "Healed!"

(John 8:12)

Let Your light reign forever in my temple!

428

The God Who Commands Wholeness, I thank You that every part of me now responds to Your authority — healed and whole!

(Mark 5:41)

Let divine command echo through my bones!

429.

The Defender of the Weak, I thank You for standing between me and the grave — You blocked it with Your blood!

(Numbers 16:48)

You are greater than the greatest — You stepped in when no one else could!

430.

The One Who Numbers My Days, I thank You that premature death has been canceled — I shall live, thrive, and overflow!

(Psalm 91:16)

Let every day ahead glorify the Healer!

431.

Jehovah El Emeth, the God of Truth, I thank You that truth swallowed every lie spoken over my health!

(John 8:32)

Let the fire of truth silence every deception!

432.

Jesus, the Finisher of My Faith, I thank You for finishing my healing story with victory, beauty, and overflow!

(Hebrews 12:2)

Let the ending be louder than the struggle!

433.

The One Who Holds the Scroll, I thank You that the script of my body is not written by man, but by You!

(Revelation 5:1–10)

Let my name be sealed with health and glory!

434.

The Prince of Peace, I thank You that torment and mental war have bowed — and peace now rules like a king!

(Isaiah 9:6)

Let shalom saturate every system within me!

435.

The Eternal Vindicator, I thank You for silencing every voice of accusation — and crowning me with divine dignity!

(Isaiah 54:17)

Let glory speak louder than shame!

436.

The Fire That Answers Altars, I thank You that my thanksgiving triggered judgment against every affliction altar!

(1 Kings 18:38)

Let fire consume what words couldn't!

437.

The One Who Blows With Wind and Fire, I thank You for releasing Your breath into my lungs and turning fatigue into fire!

(Acts 2:2–3)

Let my breath carry Pentecostal force!

438.

Jesus, the Great Physician, I thank You that Your diagnosis was mercy, and Your prescription was glory!

(Mark 2:17)

Let Heaven's medical record overrule Earth's report!

439.

The Captain of My Wholeness, I thank You for leading me out of the ICU and into divine identity!

(Exodus 15:26)

Let my discharge papers be signed by glory!

440.

Father, I thank You! The symptoms are gone. The root is destroyed. The torment is judged. And the future is flaming with strength!

Let fire stay in my blood. Let joy erupt in my soul. Let praise burn on my altar. And let healing glorify You forever!

This is not temporary — it is eternal.

Hallelujah to the God who heals and reigns forever!

441.

Jesus, the Stone Cut Without Hands, I thank You for destroying every ancient foundation of inherited disease!

(Daniel 2:34)

Let every generational altar collapse under Your power!

442.

The Voice That Splits Cedars, I thank You for shattering affliction with a whisper — You didn't even break a sweat!

(Psalm 29:5)

Praise be to God — one Word made me whole!

443.

The One Who Holds My Times, I thank You that no sickness can shorten the years You have ordained for me!

(Psalm 31:15)

Let long life speak loudly of Your covenant!

444.

The Flame of Heaven, I thank You for branding me with holy fire — sickness now fears the scent of my presence!

(Song of Solomon 8:6)

Let divine fire become my fragrance!

445.

Jesus, the Destroyer of Yokes, I thank You for destroying mental torment, body fatigue, and spiritual weariness!

(Isaiah 10:27)

Let the anointing keep me weightless in glory!

446.

The One Who Shuts the Mouth of Lions, I thank You for silencing every evil voice that said I wouldn't recover!

(Daniel 6:22)

You are greater than the greatest — You closed the mouth of death!

447.

The Cloud by Day, I thank You for covering me from every heatwave of torment — and shielding me with Your presence!

(Exodus 13:21)

Let glory be my atmosphere forever!

448.

The One Who Speaks in Fire, I thank You for speaking to every organ with creative power and supernatural precision!

(Deuteronomy 4:33)

Let every system respond to Your command!

449.

The Master of the Deep, I thank You for reaching into places no medicine could touch — and healing me by Spirit and Word!

(1 Corinthians 2:10)

Let no root remain! Let glory fill the depth!

450.

The One Who Gives Strength to the Weary, I thank You for reviving what was exhausted and recharging me like lightning!

(Isaiah 40:29)

Let divine stamina silence every former weakness!

451.

Jesus, my Open Door, I thank You that You closed the chapter of suffering and opened a scroll of celebration!

(Revelation 3:7)

Let the gate of wholeness never shut again!

452.

The Defender of the Defenseless, I thank You for fighting when I was too weak to stand, too weary to speak!

(Psalm 82:3)

God I adore You — You stepped in and won the war!

453.

The Wind in My Lungs, I thank You for giving me back my breath, my voice, my strength, and my song!

(Genesis 2:7)

Let every inhale carry worship and every exhale release fire!

454.

The One Who Keeps the Fire Burning, I thank You that my altar will never go cold — praise will never stop!

(Leviticus 6:13)

Let my thanksgiving ignite revival everywhere I go!

455.

The Thunder That Fights for Me, I thank You that while the enemy whispered, You thundered — and scattered them in pieces!

(Psalm 18:13–14)

Let divine soundwaves destroy every resistance!

456.

Jesus, my Kinsman Redeemer, I thank You for buying me back from the pit of affliction — and paying in blood!

(Ruth 4:14; Isaiah 43:1)

Hallelujah! I am redeemed, restored, and rising!

457.

The One Who Covers Me in the Night, I thank You that no night terror, no secret attack, and no hidden arrow can touch me!

(Psalm 91:5)

You are my Shield in silence and in storm!

458.

The Lord My Portion, I thank You that affliction is not my portion — healing, fire, and glory are!

(Lamentations 3:24)

Let my inheritance burn bright with praise!

459.

Jesus, the Fulfillment of All Things, I thank You that I don't need a second source — You are enough for my full healing!

(Matthew 5:17)

Praise be to God — nothing missing, nothing broken!

460.

Father, I thank You! The devil's sentence is broken, the timeline is reversed, and the root is crushed.

You replaced torment with testimony, fear with fire, and sorrow with strength.

This life, this breath, this health — it's Yours. Use it for Your glory!

Let this thanksgiving burn forever. Hallelujah to the King of Fire!

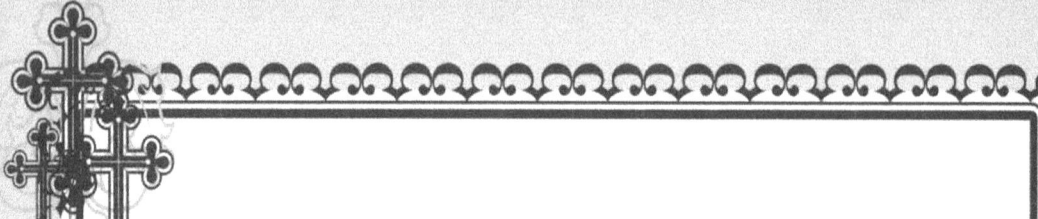

461.

Jesus, the Light of the World, I thank You that Your light exposed the darkness in my body — and burned it out completely!

(John 8:12)

Let no trace of disease ever hide again!

462.

The One Who Was and Is and Is to Come, I thank You that You've healed my past, secured my present, and sealed my future!

(Revelation 1:8)

Praise be to God — healing is timeless and eternal!

463.

The Author and Finisher, I thank You that no affliction can add a chapter You didn't write!

(Hebrews 12:2)

Let the final word be healing, fire, and praise!

464.

The Warrior With a Sword in His Mouth, I thank You for slaying every serpent of sickness with the fire of Your Word!

(Revelation 19:15)

Let Your sword keep cutting until all is silent!

465.

The Builder Who Never Fails, I thank You for rebuilding my life stronger than before — glory in every cell!

(Amos 9:11)

Let divine reconstruction shout louder than the ruins!

466.

The Name That Cannot Be Defeated, I thank You that every label of disease has bowed — and Your Name has risen!

(Philippians 2:9–11)

Hallelujah! Your Name has swallowed every diagnosis!

467.

The One Who Lays Hands from Heaven, I thank You that Your invisible touch was more effective than every treatment!

(Mark 1:41)

Let Your touch remain and never be undone!

468.

The Consuming Fire, I thank You for consuming not only symptoms but also every hidden covenant of sickness!

(Hebrews 12:29)

Let the ashes testify that the enemy is no more!

469.

The Owner of the Oil, I thank You that Your anointing didn't just flow — it flooded me with fire and freedom!

(Isaiah 10:27)

Let oil run through my bones and keep me whole!

470.

The Shepherd Who Restores My Soul, I thank You that emotional wounds have now become rivers of peace!

(Psalm 23:3)

Let the past be healed and the soul refreshed!

471.

Jesus, the Voice of Resurrection, I thank You that You called every dying cell, and they answered with life!

(John 11:43)

Let resurrection be my body's daily rhythm!

472.

The Alpha of Wholeness, I thank You that You started this healing — and You're finishing it with fire!

(Philippians 1:6)

No delay. No relapse. Only glory!

473.

The One Who Speaks Once and Ends All Battles, I thank You that You said "Healed!" and every devil went silent!

(Psalm 62:11)

Let Your voice echo through generations!

474.

The Lord My Shield, I thank You for blocking every returning arrow, monitoring eye, and familiar oppression!

(Psalm 3:3)

Let divine shields stay lifted forever!

475.

The Banner of Victory, I thank You that the flag flying over me is not defeat — but "Divine Recovery Complete!"

(Song of Songs 2:4)

Hallelujah! My identity is fire-marked!

476.

The Thunder in My Praise, I thank You for making every shout of thanks a weapon — and every whisper a sword!

(Psalm 149:6–9)

Let my praise be heard in the spirit realm!

477.

The One Who Holds the Scroll of My Life, I thank You that my healing was already written — and it cannot be undone!

(Psalm 139:16)

Let the scroll speak louder than symptoms!

478.

Jesus, My Dwelling Place, I thank You that You've become my immunity, my medicine, and my fireproof shelter!

(Psalm 91:1)

Let my hiding place be glory upon glory!

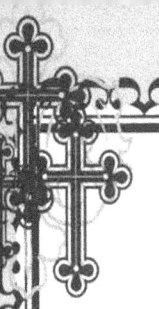

479.

The One Who Turned My Night into Day, I thank You for flipping every dark diagnosis into divine demonstration!

(Psalm 30:5)

Let the sunrise of healing never set again!

480.

Father, I thank You! You've left no part untouched, no issue unaddressed, no sickness undefeated.

Let this temple now serve You with fire, with joy, and with unshakable praise.

The war is over. The victory is written. The glory is Yours forever!

Hallelujah to the King of Healing and Flame!

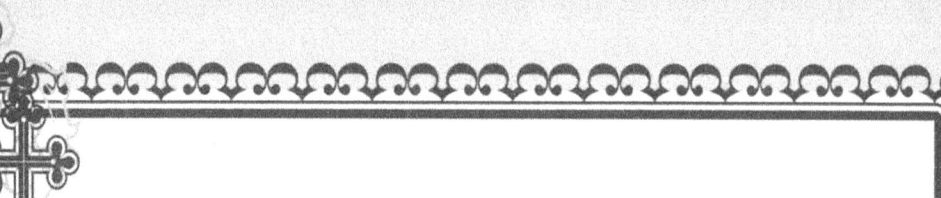

481.

Jesus, the One Who Was Wounded for Me, I thank You that every stripe on Your back sealed my healing forever!

(Isaiah 53:5)

Let no wound survive the power of Your sacrifice!

482.

The Fire That Consumes All Disease, I thank You that every cell in my body is now too hot for affliction to rest!

(Hebrews 12:29)

Let Your fire be my immune system forever!

483.

Jehovah Rapha, the God Who Heals Me, I thank You for healing what doctors couldn't explain and restoring what man couldn't fix!

(Exodus 15:26)

You are greater than the greatest — and I live to tell it!

484.

The Voice That Called Me Out, I thank You for pulling me out of the pit, the pain, and the prognosis!

(Psalm 40:2)

Let my name be known in Heaven as "testimony!"

485.

Jesus, the Lamb Who Was Slain, I thank You that Your blood bought my freedom from every affliction, visible or hidden!

(Revelation 5:9)

Let Your blood speak louder than every accusation!

486.

The God of Turnarounds, I thank You that my worst diagnosis became my greatest praise!

(Genesis 50:20)

Let the devil be permanently disappointed!

487

The One Who Opens and No One Can Shut, I thank You that You opened the door of divine health and shut the gate of affliction!

(Revelation 3:7–8)

Let permanent doors of wholeness stay open forever!

488.

The One Who Fights While I Worship, I thank You that every "hallelujah" released angels to war on my behalf!

(2 Chronicles 20:22)

Let my thanksgiving be a fire-sword in the spirit!

489.

The Potter Who Reformed Me, I thank You for reshaping what was cracked, realigning what was twisted, and restoring what was broken!

(Jeremiah 18:4)

God I adore You — I am glory-made, fire-sealed!

490.

The Spirit That Raised Jesus, I thank You that resurrection power is active in my body daily — keeping me alive, alert, and unstoppable!

(Romans 8:11)

Let every day carry the force of Your empty tomb!

491.

The One Who Carries Me, I thank You that in moments of weakness, You became my legs, my lungs, my strength, and my shout!

(Isaiah 46:4)

Let my strength remain supernatural — forever!

492.

The One Who Preserves My Bones, I thank You that not one has been broken, and none shall decay!

(Psalm 34:20)

Let my skeletal system praise You daily!

493.

Jesus, the Great Exchange, I thank You that You took my sorrow and gave me songs, took my weakness and gave me wonder!

(Isaiah 61:3)

Let every part of me reflect divine trade-in glory!

494.

The Fire That Answers Praise, I thank You that when I lifted my voice, You responded with holy fire!

(2 Chronicles 7:1)

Let my praise forever remain flammable!

495.

The Breath of the Almighty, I thank You that every breath I take now carries purpose, power, and presence!

(Job 33:4)

Let every inhale be revival, every exhale be glory!

496.

The God of Completion, I thank You that You didn't just begin my healing — You brought it to finality!

(Ecclesiastes 3:14)

Let no residue, no fragment, no fear remain!

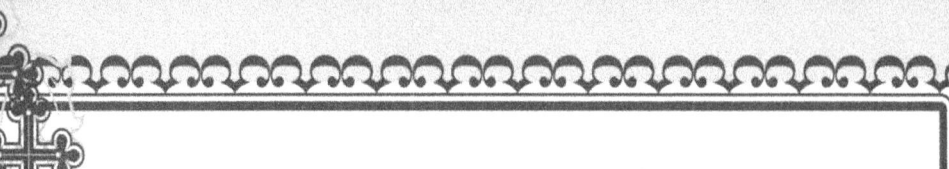

497.

Jesus, the One Who Gives Joy Instead of Mourning, I thank You for restoring laughter to my soul and dancing to my feet!

(Psalm 30:11)

Let my movements become worship!

498.

The Thunder That Silences Hell, I thank You that Your voice sent confusion into every demonic assignment!

(Psalm 29:3–9)

Let hell remain in permanent silence over my life!

499.

The King Who Took My Place, I thank You that judgment passed over me because it landed on You!

(Isaiah 53:6)

Let the finished work of Calvary echo through my bloodline!

500.

Father, I thank You! You didn't just touch me — You transformed me. You didn't just heal me — You made me a weapon. You didn't just restore me — You reintroduced me.

This fire is permanent. This healing is unbreakable. This praise is my identity forever.

Let every breath shout Your Name. Let every step march in victory. Let every season drip with fire.

Hallelujah to the God who leaves no trace of sickness behind!

501.

Jesus, my Avenger, I thank You for silencing every altar that claimed my body and burning their records with holy fire!

(Psalm 94:1)

Let vengeance be final, loud, and glorious!

502.

The Resurrection and the Life, I thank You for resurrecting my strength, my dreams, my joy, and my fire!

(John 11:25)

Hallelujah! Let every dry bone live again!

503.

The God Who Sees and Acts, I thank You that You didn't just observe my pain — You invaded it with fire and freedom!

(Exodus 3:7–8)

God I adore You — You moved when others watched!

504.

The Consuming Fire, I thank You that not one germ, root, pattern, or voice of sickness escaped Your judgment!

(Deuteronomy 4:24)

Let the smoke of victory rise continually!

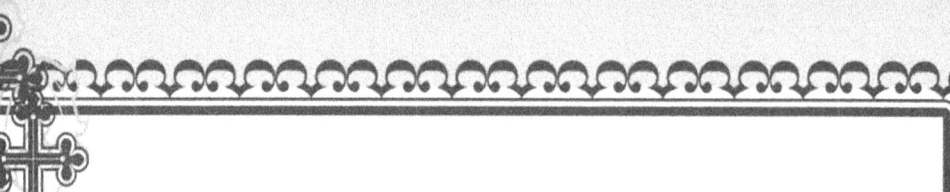

505.

The Healer With No Expiration, I thank You that this testimony won't fade — my healing is eternal and irreversible!

(Hebrews 13:8)

You are greater than the greatest — always faithful!

506.

Jesus, the Defender of My Destiny, I thank You for shielding the purpose You placed in me from the claws of affliction!

(Jeremiah 1:5)

Let every assignment You wrote come alive in strength!

507.

The One Who Restores Faster Than Time, I thank You that what took years to break down, You rebuilt in moments!

(Isaiah 58:12)

Let speed, fire, and strength define my recovery!

508.

The God of Surprise Victories, I thank You for ambushing the enemy and turning my groan into glory!

(2 Chronicles 20:22)

Let my worship remain a divine trap for darkness!

509.

The Repairer of Glory, I thank You for covering the shame of affliction with dignity, splendor, and power!

(Zechariah 3:4)

Let my story be too glorious to ignore!

510.

The One Who Carries My Frame, I thank You for reinforcing every weak place and building me into an unshakable temple!

(Isaiah 46:4)

Let the strength of Zion rest upon me forever!

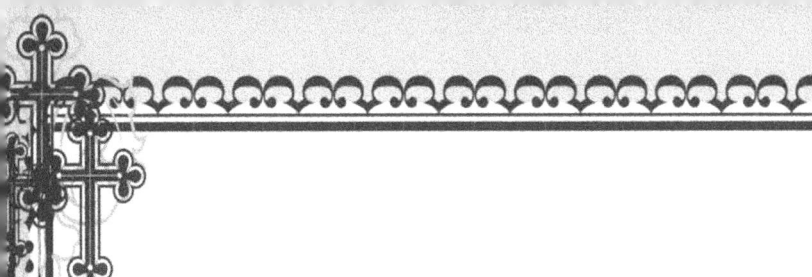

511.

Jesus, the Anchor That Holds, I thank You for holding me when waves of fear and diagnosis tried to pull me under!

(Hebrews 6:19)

Let Your grip on my soul never loosen!

512.

The Voice That Ends Battles, I thank You that You didn't argue with sickness — You commanded it to go, and it fled!

(Mark 1:25)

Let every remaining symptom vanish by fire!

513.

The One Who Never Fails, I thank You for coming through when all other systems said, "Prepare for the worst."

(Psalm 73:26)

You are the last word — and it is good!

514.

The Fire That Burns Backward, I thank You that You even healed the damage of yesterday — no history shall haunt me!

(Joel 2:25)

Let retroactive fire restore everything!

515.

Jesus, the Champion of My Body, I thank You that my organs respond better to Your voice than to prescriptions!

(Luke 4:36)

Let divine obedience continue in every cell!

516.

The Giver of Songs in the Night, I thank You for turning silent cries into joyful declarations of praise!

(Psalm 42:8)

Let melody replace mourning — forever!

517.

The Builder of the Broken, I thank You that where others saw weakness, You saw a house for fire and praise!

(Isaiah 61:4)

Let every ruin become a platform of testimony!

518.

Jesus, the Final Gatekeeper, I thank You for locking the gate behind my past and throwing the key into the fire!

(Revelation 3:7)

No reentry for affliction — only forward with glory!

519.

The Keeper of My Oil, I thank You for ensuring my lamp never runs dry — praise, strength, and vision stay full!

(Matthew 25:4)

Let the flame stay high and the altar stay hot!

520.

Father, I thank You! Every scar has become a sign. Every battle has birthed boldness. Every storm has produced fire.

You didn't just heal me — You baptized me with unquenchable praise.

From now until eternity, this temple shall glorify You in joy, fire, and power!

Hallelujah to the King of my healing, forever!

521.

Jesus, the One Who Called Me Out, I thank You for calling me out of affliction with authority and crowning me with glory!

(Luke 13:12)

Let Your call echo through every cell of my body!

522.

The Fire That Goes Before Me, I thank You that You've burned every demonic ambush before it could reach me!

(Deuteronomy 9:3)

Let every trap melt in the heat of Your presence!

523.

The God Who Seals My Testimony, I thank You that no counterattack, whisper, or scheme can reverse what You have finished!

(Ephesians 1:13)

Let this healing be irreversible by fire!

524.

The Owner of My Destiny, I thank You that sickness cannot hijack my journey — Your plan prevails!

(Jeremiah 29:11)

Let affliction miss every appointment in my future!

525.

Jesus, the Lord of the Sabbath, I thank You for giving me rest in areas I once wrestled — body, mind, and soul!

(Matthew 11:28)

Let rest flow like a river through every part of me!

526.

The Fire That Cannot Be Quenched, I thank You for igniting thanksgiving that cannot be silenced — not now, not ever!

(Leviticus 6:13)

Let this altar of praise burn until eternity!

527.

The One Who Commands Healing, I thank You for speaking life into me and watching every symptom obey!

(Psalm 107:20)

Let Your command echo in my bloodstream daily!

528.

The Lord My Banner, I thank You for flying the flag of victory over my health — forever lifted, never lowered!

(Exodus 17:15)

Let the banner of healing wave in every season!

529.

Jesus, the Flame in My Bones, I thank You for filling me with holy fire — fatigue has no seat left!

(Jeremiah 20:9)

Let divine energy overtake every weakness!

530.

The Breaker of Delay, I thank You that what lingered for years ended in moments when You showed up!

(Isaiah 48:3)

Hallelujah! Speed and fire now define my journey!

531.

The God Who Finishes What He Starts, I thank You that no unfinished healing remains — everything is complete in You!

(Philippians 1:6)

Let the final touches be marked with eternal fire!

532.

Jesus, the Key Holder, I thank You for unlocking my future and locking the doors of pain and disease behind me!

(Revelation 3:7)

Let affliction be locked out for good!

533.

The One Who Inhabits Praise, I thank You that as I thanked You, You filled my body with divine presence!

(Psalm 22:3)

Let Your glory stay in every organ and every breath!

534.

The Fire That Fights For Me, I thank You that even when I was quiet, the fire kept burning, and the war kept winning!

(Exodus 14:14)

You are greater than the greatest — You fought and finished it!

535.

The Architect of Wholeness, I thank You for designing my recovery with beauty, strength, and no side effects!

(Isaiah 58:11)

Let divine architecture rebuild what was ruined!

536.

The One Who Never Sleeps, I thank You that while I rested, You were reprogramming my systems for perfect health!

(Psalm 121:4)

Let my rest be filled with restoration!

537.

The Eternal Light, I thank You that no darkness of sickness could remain under the weight of Your presence!

(John 1:5)

Let the light stay on forever in my temple!

538.

Jesus, my Victory Shout, I thank You that every time I said "Thank You," You said "Done!"

(2 Chronicles 20:22)

Let my shout keep shaking hell!

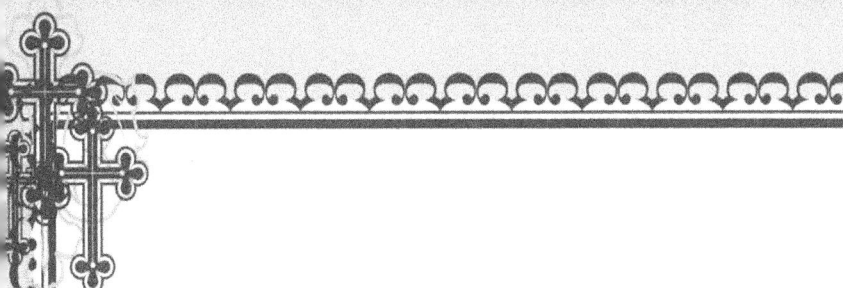

539.

The Giver of New Beginnings, I thank You that my life has started over — fresh body, fresh mind, fresh fire!

(Isaiah 43:19)

Let everything ahead be brighter than what I left!

540.

The Lord Who Is Mighty to Save, I thank You for saving me completely — not partially, not temporarily, but eternally!

(Isaiah 63:1)

Hallelujah! Let wholeness be my new identity!

541.

The One Who Carries My Name, I thank You that sickness cannot rename me — my name is Healed, Anointed, and Rising!

(Isaiah 62:2)

Let Heaven and Earth know I've been marked by glory!

542.

The Living Water, I thank You for flooding my dry places with strength, stamina, and supernatural recovery!

(John 7:38)

Let Your river keep flowing through every fiber of me!

543.

Jesus, the Thunder Above My Enemies, I thank You for answering every whisper of the enemy with a roar from glory!

(Psalm 18:13)

Let divine thunder remain my background sound!

544.

The Flame on My Altar, I thank You for turning my thanksgiving into warfare — every hallelujah is now a weapon!

(Psalm 149:6)

Let my mouth stay on fire with praise!

545.

The God Who Lifts the Humble, I thank You for exalting me from the place of affliction into a throne of testimony!

(1 Peter 5:6)

Let my seat of healing never be vacated!

546.

The Promise Keeper, I thank You that not one Word failed — what You said, You did, and You sealed with fire!

(Numbers 23:19)

Praise be to the God whose promises are permanent!

547.

The One Who Hears Every Whisper, I thank You that even in silence, You were preparing glory for my story!

(Romans 8:26)

Let my still moments be filled with divine action!

548.

Jesus, the Reward of the Faithful, I thank You that what I believed, I have now received — pressed down and blazing!

(Hebrews 11:6)

Let this healing be the down payment of greater glory!

549.

The One Who Never Lost a Battle, I thank You that my body is now part of Your record of victories!

(2 Chronicles 20:15)

Let the record of triumph never stop increasing!

550.

Father, I thank You! My body is no longer a battlefield — it is a throne room. No pain remains. No whisper remains. No fear remains.

Only glory. Only fire. Only You. Let this thanksgiving become my song forever.

Let every cell declare: The Lord has done this — and it is marvelous in our sight!

551.

Jesus, my Defender and King, I thank You for silencing every voice of accusation that rose against my health!

(Isaiah 54:17)

Let every evil word melt in the heat of Your justice!

552.

The One Who Overthrows Thrones, I thank You for toppling every illegal altar where sickness was being renewed!

(Jeremiah 1:10)

Let destruction rest upon every root of affliction!

553.

The Glory That Covers Me, I thank You for wrapping me in divine fire — I'm no longer vulnerable, I'm untouchable!

(Isaiah 4:5)

Let Your flame be my clothing forever!

554.

The Fire That Spoke for Me, I thank You for letting Your presence plead my case when my strength ran out!

(Romans 8:26)

Let divine intercession speak louder than pain!

555.

The Eternal Healer, I thank You that my healing isn't seasonal — it's secured, sealed, and settled by Your covenant!

(Psalm 89:34)

Let Your Word remain the law in my body!

556.

Jesus, the Root and Offspring of David, I thank You for replanting my life in strength, wholeness, and fire!

(Revelation 22:16)

Let nothing weak grow again in this soil!

557.

The Author of My Wholeness, I thank You for finishing the book of affliction and opening the scroll of divine recovery!

(Psalm 139:16)

Let my next chapters carry only glory!

558.

The Fire of Pentecost, I thank You for filling me with supernatural boldness, energy, and unshakable joy!

(Acts 2:3–4)

Let my strength increase daily by Your flame!

559.

The One Who Erased My Shame, I thank You that where I once feared death, I now testify of deliverance!

(Psalm 34:5)

Let beauty cover every former place of mourning!

560.

The Lifter of My Spirit, I thank You for elevating me out of dark valleys and setting my feet on a mountain of praise!

(Psalm 40:2–3)

Let my new height glorify Your mercy!

561.

Jesus, my Perfect Peace, I thank You that chaos can no longer rule my thoughts, emotions, or body!

(Isaiah 26:3)

Let peace patrol every system with fire!

562.

The One Who Washes Me Clean, I thank You for flushing every trace of hidden infirmity from my inner man!

(1 John 1:7)

Let the cleansing continue forever in glory!

563.

The King Over Time, I thank You for redeeming my lost years of health — I receive divine speed in Jesus' name!

(Joel 2:25)

Let what was delayed become accelerated deliverance!

564.

The God of Completion, I thank You that I don't have to wonder if I'm healed — the answer is already YES in fire!

(Ecclesiastes 3:14)

Let completeness be loud in my testimony!

565.

The One Who Delivered Me in Silence, I thank You for fighting while I wept, for healing while I rested!

(Exodus 14:14)

Let every tear be turned into celebration!

566.

The Great Shepherd, I thank You for pulling me out of affliction and carrying me into pastures of peace!

(Psalm 23:1–3)

Let green seasons never end in my life!

567.

The One Who Dances Over Me, I thank You for rejoicing over my healing with singing and laughter!

(Zephaniah 3:17)

Let Heaven's joy be louder than hell's attempt!

568.

The Anchor of My Soul, I thank You for keeping me grounded when sickness tried to toss me like a wave!

(Hebrews 6:19)

Let Your stability hold me through every season!

569.

The One Who Burns to the Root, I thank You that no symptom, no pain, and no enemy survived Your judgment fire!

(Matthew 3:10–12)

Let the axe and the flame finish what they started!

570.

Father, I thank You! The enemy is buried. The affliction is ashes. The altar of praise is burning.

This healing is final. This strength is holy. This fire is generational.

Let the next breath be stronger. Let the next praise be louder. Let this victory never end.

Hallelujah to the One who heals, keeps, and reigns forever!

571.

Jesus, the God Who Keeps Watch, I thank You for shielding me from attacks I never saw — and healing what I didn't know was broken!

(Psalm 121:5)

Let divine surveillance guard my future forever!

572.

The One Who Speaks With Fire, I thank You that one Word from You canceled years of warfare and pain!

(Jeremiah 23:29)

Let every lie vanish in the heat of Your voice!

573.

The High Priest of My Confession, I thank You for honoring every declaration of faith I've spoken with holy fire!

(Hebrews 3:1)

Let my tongue remain a throne of praise!

574.

The Healer of Foundations, I thank You that You didn't just fix what was seen — You rebuilt me from the root with glory!

(Isaiah 58:12)

Let nothing broken remain, even in the secret places!

575.

Jesus, the Lamb Whose Blood Speaks, I thank You that Your blood is still louder than diagnosis, curses, and time!

(Hebrews 12:24)

Let the blood speak forever on my behalf!

576.

The One Who Holds the Keys, I thank You that You've locked sickness out of my story — permanently!

(Revelation 3:7)

Let only healing and strength walk through my gates!

577.

The God Who Covers Me, I thank You that no arrow, no spirit, and no sentence has power over Your protection!

(Psalm 91:4)

Let Your wings be my fireproof shelter!

578.

The Strength of My Days, I thank You that I wake up with supernatural stamina and go to bed wrapped in praise!

(Deuteronomy 33:25)

Let every day testify: "The Lord sustains me!"

579.

The One Who Broke the Chain, I thank You for breaking cycles of relapse, delay, and silent suffering!

(Nahum 1:9)

Let every chain stay buried in fire!

580.

The Fire on My Tongue, I thank You that my thanksgiving has become a weapon — destroying what pain tried to plant!

(Psalm 149:6)

Let praise continue to war on my behalf!

581.

Jesus, the Resurrection in My Veins, I thank You that Your power flows through every part of me — nothing dying, everything alive!

(Romans 8:11)

Let resurrection fire govern my entire body!

582.

The One Who Restores What Was Stolen, I thank You for giving me back what I didn't even realize I lost!

(Proverbs 6:31)

Let recovery overflow in joy, strength, and years!

583.

The Breaker of Barrenness, I thank You for breaking every medical limitation and speaking fruitfulness over my life!

(Genesis 18:14)

Let every "no" be turned into glory's "yes!"

584.

The One Who Wrote My End, I thank You that affliction will never write my last chapter — only You will!

(Psalm 139:16)

Let the conclusion be praise, not pain!

585.

Jesus, the Mighty Warrior, I thank You for defeating battles I didn't even know I was in — You are faithful!

(Exodus 15:3)

Let the unseen victories be louder than visible attacks!

586.

The One Who Commands the Morning, I thank You that my mornings are now filled with laughter, strength, and light!

(Job 38:12)

Let every sunrise speak of a healed body!

587.

The Giver of Good and Perfect Gifts, I thank You that divine health is not borrowed — it is mine by covenant!

(James 1:17)

Let no thief steal this inheritance again!

588.

The One Who Sings Over Me, I thank You that my healing was serenaded by Heaven before I saw it!

(Zephaniah 3:17)

Let Your song play forever in my spirit!

589.

The Lord Who Strengthens My Hands, I thank You for empowering me to do what I couldn't before — with fire and joy!

(Psalm 18:34)

Let every action glorify the One who restored me!

590.

Father, I thank You! What once broke me now builds me. What once shamed me now glorifies You. What once drained me now fuels revival.

Let every part of my being remain fire-filled. Let this healing be a launching pad for others. Let thanksgiving be the sound that never stops.

Hallelujah to the God who heals forever!

591.

Jesus, the God Who Interrupts Darkness, I thank You that when the enemy planned more attacks, You interrupted with power!

(Acts 9:3–4)

Let divine intervention continue to scatter every plan!

592.

The Giver of Recovery With Interest, I thank You that I'm not just healed — I've come out stronger, wiser, and full of fire!

(Zechariah 9:12)

Let my gain outweigh my pain forever!

593.

The Defender of My Days, I thank You that premature death missed me, and divine life overtook me!

(Psalm 118:17)

Let long life carry praise in every breath!

594.

The One Who Heals the Healer, I thank You that even when I poured out for others, You refilled me with fire!

(Jeremiah 30:17)

Let the overflow continue without end!

595.

Jesus, the Crown of My Head, I thank You that You removed shame, placed honor, and declared me healed!

(Isaiah 61:3)

Let royalty replace every trace of pain!

596.

The Fire That Rewrites History, I thank You that my family tree no longer carries disease — it carries testimony!

(Galatians 3:13–14)

Let my bloodline become a healing altar!

597.

The Breath That Never Fails, I thank You that every inhale is praise and every exhale is power!

(Job 33:4)

Let breath never again carry fear or fatigue!

598.

The One Who Surrounds Me, I thank You that angels now patrol my body, my home, and my tomorrow!

(Psalm 91:11)

Let divine security never be broken!

599.

The Keeper of My Covenant, I thank You that You are faithful even when I'm faint — healing is my portion by promise!

(Deuteronomy 7:9)

Let covenant fire protect what You've established!

600.

Father, I thank You! You've carried me through battles I didn't announce and wars I didn't understand.

You healed the deep places. You restored the hidden places. You reign over every inch of me.

Let every cell, every memory, every system declare: "Jesus reigns here — sickness has no seat."

This temple is Yours. This altar is Yours. This testimony is eternal.

Hallelujah!

601.

Jesus, the Strength of My Days, I thank You that from morning to night, fire surrounds my body and sustains my spirit!

(Deuteronomy 33:25)

Let every hour testify that I am kept by Your glory!

602.

The One Who Overthrew the Curse, I thank You that the chain of generational sickness has been shattered once and for all!

(Galatians 3:13)

Let every future generation walk in this fire!

603.

The God Who Answers Before I Call, I thank You that You healed me before I even finished crying out!

(Isaiah 65:24)

Let Your mercy outrun every attack of the enemy!

604.

Jesus, the Surgeon of Heaven, I thank You for operating on what man couldn't reach and restoring what man couldn't find!

(Jeremiah 30:17)

Let Your hands remain on my life forever!

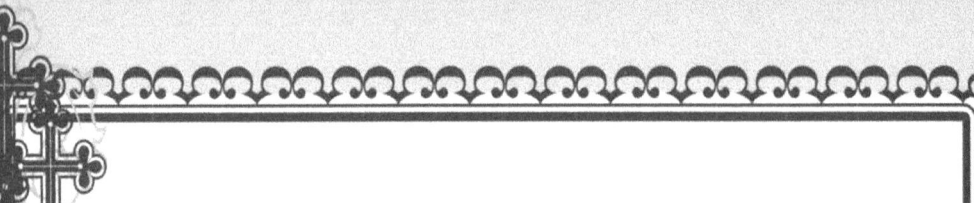

605.

The Fire That Watches My Gates, I thank You that no old affliction can reenter — every exit is sealed with fire!

(Psalm 127:1)

Let my body be guarded by divine flame!

606.

The Giver of Unexplainable Strength, I thank You for letting me do more than I ever imagined — with ease and joy!

(Philippians 4:13)

Let this new strength become my daily song!

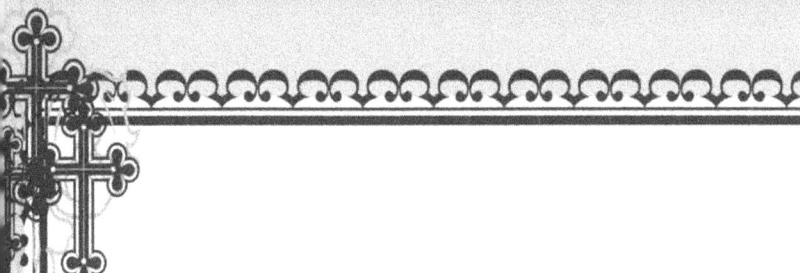

607.

The One Who Commands Peace, I thank You for commanding stillness into my bloodstream, bones, and breath!

(Mark 4:39)

Let nothing ever disturb this covenant peace!

608.

The Fire on My Tongue, I thank You for turning my thanksgiving into prophecy, and my voice into a healing river!

(Proverbs 18:21)

Let my words always glorify the One who healed me!

609.

The God Who Redeems Time, I thank You for restoring the years I spent under affliction — and multiplying what's ahead!

(Joel 2:25)

Let fire overtake every wasted season!

610.

The One Who Seals My Testimony, I thank You that this healing is eternal — no devil, no time, no lie can undo it!

(Ephesians 1:13)

Let divine proof follow me all my days!

611.

Jesus, the Flame That Keeps Burning, I thank You that the fire on this altar will never go out — not in my body, not in my generations!

(Leviticus 6:13)

Let praise be my permanent incense and protection!

612.

The One Who Tramples Serpents, I thank You that every evil monitor, whisper, or watcher of sickness has been crushed underfoot!

(Luke 10:19)

Let no snake rise again — Your Word is final!

613.

The Author of Life, I thank You that no unauthorized sentence can be written over my health — You hold the pen!

(Acts 3:15)

Let my story be sealed by the blood of Jesus!

614.

The One Who Rebuilds What Was Torn, I thank You that my systems have been rebuilt with glory, not just recovery!

(Amos 9:11)

Let divine architecture outlast every old report!

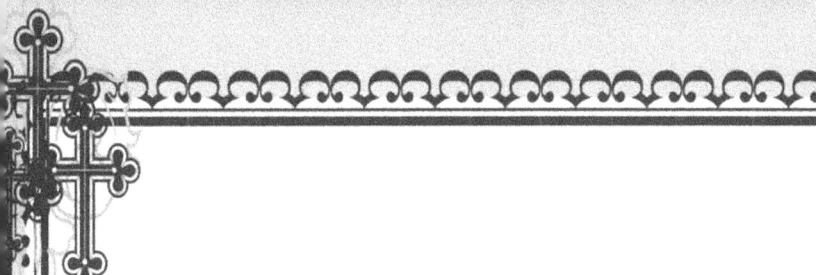

615.

Jehovah Nissi, my Banner, I thank You that every time I lift my hands in praise, You send fire into the camp of my enemies!

(Exodus 17:15)

Let thanksgiving continue to be my sword and shield!

616.

The God Who Turns Mourning into Dancing, I thank You that the days of heaviness are over — I rise in color, strength, and joy!

(Psalm 30:11)

Let joy dance louder than pain ever screamed!

617.

The Builder of My Immune System, I thank You that my body is now reinforced with supernatural durability!

(Psalm 139:14)

Let divine resistance remain unshakable within me!

618.

Jesus, the God of My Mountains, I thank You that no matter how high the diagnosis seemed, You spoke and it crumbled!

(Mark 11:23)

Let every obstacle remember the voice that silenced it!

619.

The Everlasting Father, I thank You that my healing isn't based on time, age, or stage — it's based on Your eternal promise!

(Isaiah 9:6)

Let age never reduce what glory has restored!

620.

Father, I thank You! The case is closed. The blood has spoken. The fire has fallen. The temple is whole.

Let nothing unclean return. Let no pain whisper again. Let no voice rise above the Name of Jesus.

My life is healed. My testimony is sealed. My praise is forever!

Hallelujah

621.

Jesus, the Great Physician, I thank You for completing the work — not one issue escaped Your healing touch!

(Matthew 9:35)

Let Your wholeness reign from head to toe!

622.

The One Who Cancels Verdicts, I thank You that every judgment of affliction has been torn, reversed, and buried!

(Colossians 2:14)

Let no sentence be spoken again — the case is closed!

623.

The Fire That Covers Me, I thank You for creating a barrier of glory around my life — no more invasion, no more torment!

(Zechariah 2:5)

Let Your presence continue to be my wall!

624.

The Giver of Divine Endurance, I thank You that I run and don't grow weary, I walk and do not faint!

(Isaiah 40:31)

Let energy from Heaven flow daily in my frame!

625.

Jesus, the One Who Shook Hell for Me, I thank You that what once bound me is now broken under Your feet!

(Revelation 1:18)

Let every chain remain in pieces!

626.

The Light That Destroys Darkness, I thank You that every shadow of illness has disappeared under Your flame!

(John 1:5)

Let every corner of my being remain lit by glory!

627.

The One Who Brings Me Out, I thank You for bringing me out of the furnace stronger than I entered it!

(Daniel 3:27)

Let preservation become my identity forever!

628.

The God Who Removes Reproach, I thank You that shame from my past health battles has turned into a platform of praise!

(Joshua 5:9)

Let my healing honor Your name before the nations!

629.

The Thunder in My Silence, I thank You that even when I had no strength to pray, my faith still spoke fire!

(Romans 8:26)

Let my quiet tears now thunder with thanksgiving!

630.

The One Who Fills My Mouth, I thank You that my lips now flow with praise, not complaint — worship, not weakness!

(Psalm 34:1)

Let every word from my mouth burn with gratitude!

631.

The Breaker of Limits, I thank You for destroying medical limits and placing me in supernatural recovery zones!

(Mark 5:26–29)

Let every record be broken by Your glory!

632.

Jesus, my Spiritual Fortress, I thank You that my mind, emotions, and body are now safe from demonic manipulation!

(Proverbs 18:10)

Let divine fortification guard me forever!

633.

The Fire That Swallowed the Enemy, I thank You that the enemy was swallowed whole — not just silenced, but erased!

(Exodus 15:4–6)

Let my victory be a memorial of Your greatness!

634.

The God of All Grace, I thank You for replacing frustration with favor and pain with praise!

(1 Peter 5:10)

Let grace govern every step I take forward!

635.

The One Who Does Great Things Without Number, I thank You that my recovery is full of wonders I can't even count!

(Job 5:9)

Let miracle after miracle mark my journey!

636.

The Healer Who Walks With Me, I thank You that healing is not just an event — it's a Person walking beside me daily!

(Isaiah 41:10)

Let this companionship of glory never end!

637.

The One Who Restores Honor, I thank You that I will never be mocked by sickness again — You have covered me in dignity!

(Isaiah 61:7)

Let restoration roar louder than every insult!

638.

Jesus, my Defender Day and Night, I thank You that while I sleep, You stand guard over every system in my body!

(Psalm 121:3–4)

Let midnight become a moment of miracles!

639.

The God of Uninterrupted Praise, I thank You that nothing will mute my mouth again — not fear, not pain, not shame!

(Psalm 149:6)

Let my voice become a trumpet of power!

640.

Father, I thank You! You've walked me through the fire, through the fight, and into freedom.

Let this freedom never be quiet. Let this fire never die. Let this thanksgiving never stop.

The enemy is defeated. The glory remains. And my healing is Your forever testimony.

Hallelujah to the King who heals completely!

641.

Jesus, the One Who Satisfies Me Early, I thank You that I didn't have to wait for healing — You came right on time!

(Psalm 90:14)

Let early deliverance be my covenant forever!

642.

The King Who Breaks Protocol, I thank You that what took others years, You did for me in moments!

(Mark 2:12)

Let divine speed override every delay!

643.

The Keeper of My Record, I thank You that every scar has been transformed into a seal of victory!

(Psalm 56:8)

Let my wounds become wonders in Your glory!

644.

The Consuming Fire, I thank You that even microscopic remnants of disease were not spared — You cleansed me completely!

(Malachi 4:1–2)

Let the flame continue to burn beneath the surface!

645.

The God of Overflow, I thank You that I am not just healed — I am strengthened, restored, and saturated in glory!

(John 10:10)

Let abundance mark every step forward!

646.

The Lord Who Settles Me, I thank You for settling my health battle once and for all — no return, no reversal!

(1 Peter 5:10)

Let fire protect what You've established!

647.

Jesus, the Intercessor of Heaven, I thank You that You prayed for me until power rose again in my body!

(Luke 22:32)

Let my strength be permanent and unstoppable!

648.

The God Who Opens My Eyes, I thank You for helping me see that I was never alone — You were fighting for me all along!

(2 Kings 6:17)

Let the awareness of glory fuel my worship forever!

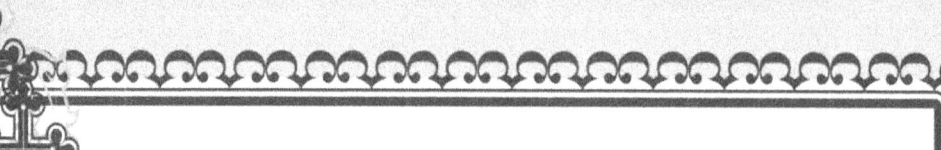

649.

The One Who Declares Me Clean, I thank You for not just touching me — but calling me whole, worthy, and fire-covered!

(Luke 5:13)

Let the label "Healed" never be removed again!

650.

The Fountain of Living Waters, I thank You that no dryness, drought, or fatigue can survive Your flow through my life!

(John 4:14)

Let rivers of healing never stop flowing within me!

651.

The One Who Restores My Soul, I thank You for healing wounds no one could see and replacing pain with peace!

(Psalm 23:3)

Let every memory be washed in fire and joy!

652.

Jesus, my Defender at the Gate, I thank You for standing watch where I was once vulnerable — now glory is my gatekeeper!

(Isaiah 60:18)

Let my entrances and exits be guarded by flame!

653.

The God Who Called Me Out, I thank You for pulling me out of the waiting room of affliction and into the throne room of glory!

(1 Peter 2:9)

Let my life reflect the light of deliverance!

654.

The One Who Shakes the Nations, I thank You that even the systems that supported my affliction were shaken down!

(Haggai 2:6–7)

Let only what is fire-approved remain in me!

655.

The Lord Who Commands Health, I thank You for speaking to my systems with divine authority — and watching them obey!

(Deuteronomy 28:8)

Let every command continue to manifest in power!

656.

Jesus, the Anointed One, I thank You that Your anointing broke every yoke and filled me with resurrection strength!

(Isaiah 10:27)

Let Your oil drip daily from head to toe!

657.

The God Who Despises Shame, I thank You for turning hidden battles into public testimonies!

(Hebrews 12:2)

Let the stage of healing reflect the power of Heaven!

658.

The One Who Speaks Better Things, I thank You that the blood still speaks — and its words are louder than diagnosis!

(Hebrews 12:24)

Let the volume of redemption never be silenced!

659.

The Eternal Flame on My Altar, I thank You for turning this body into a temple that burns with praise and power!

(1 Corinthians 6:19–20)

Let glory remain my permanent atmosphere!

660.

Father, I thank You! You did what no one else could do, touched what no one else could reach, healed what no one else could name.

From diagnosis to declaration, from battle to banner, from weakness to worship — You alone did it!

Let this thanksgiving live longer than the affliction ever did. Let Your Name be praised forever!

Hallelujah to the Healer of all things!

661.

Jesus, the Restorer of My Joy, I thank You that You didn't just heal my body — You healed my smile, my voice, and my vision!

(Psalm 126:2)

Let joy overflow and never run dry!

662.

The God Who Declares the End From the Beginning, I thank You that this affliction had an end date — and it expired in fire!

(Isaiah 46:10)

Let no evil timeline be extended in my life again!

663.

The One Who Binds Up My Wounds, I thank You that nothing is left open — physically, spiritually, or emotionally!

(Psalm 147:3)

Let sealed places now serve as praise altars!

664.

The Fire That Judges the Hidden, I thank You for rooting out affliction that was buried and silencing what was cycling!

(Luke 8:17)

Let nothing survive that You didn't plant!

665.

Jesus, the Fountain That Never Fails, I thank You for constantly pouring healing into my daily life!

(John 7:38)

Let rivers of glory flood every new day!

666.

The One Who Fought While I Slept, I thank You that while I rested, angels warred and glory won!

(Psalm 121:4)

Let midnight miracles keep manifesting in my life!

667.

The Covenant Keeper, I thank You for remembering every Word You spoke over me — and performing them with fire!

(Numbers 23:19)

Let covenant fulfillment never be delayed again!

668.

Jesus, the God of My Health, I thank You for personally taking over my case and turning it into a miracle!

(Jeremiah 30:17)

Let Heaven's report silence Earth's diagnosis forever!

669.

The One Who Restores Like a Flood, I thank You that You didn't just restore — You overwhelmed me with victory!

(Isaiah 59:19)

Let the flood of fire overtake everything I lost!

670.

The Lord Who Gives Peace Beyond Understanding, I thank You that I now sleep in peace, wake up in strength, and walk in fire!

(Philippians 4:7)

Let peace guard me like armor!

671.

Jesus, the One Who Rewrites Stories, I thank You for erasing tragedy and writing triumph in permanent glory!

(Isaiah 43:18–19)

Let every chapter ahead declare deliverance!

672.

The Lifter of My Name, I thank You that people now see Your power in me — not pain, not pity, but proof!

(Psalm 18:48)

Let Your reputation ride on my recovery!

673.

The Breath That Strengthens Me, I thank You that every breath I take is charged with glory — not weakness!

(Genesis 2:7)

Let divine oxygen keep flowing into my lungs!

674.

The Fire That Consumes Sickness, I thank You that affliction can't rest here — my life is too hot, too holy, too sealed!

(Hebrews 12:29)

Let every symptom burn before it even begins!

675.

The One Who Restores Double, I thank You that You gave me more than what I lost — You upgraded me with fire!

(Job 42:10)

Let double be my new portion from now on!

676.

The One Who Sees the Secret Place, I thank You for healing what I was too afraid to speak out loud!

(Matthew 6:6)

Let Your mercy flood every hidden scar!

677.

The Giver of Strength to the Faint, I thank You for refueling me until weakness became worship!

(Isaiah 40:29)

Let fire fill every area once called "tired!"

678.

The One Who Keeps My Feet From Slipping, I thank You that my path is now guarded — no setback, no relapse!

(Psalm 121:3)

Let healing stand tall where I once fell!

679.

Jesus, the Song in My Night, I thank You that even in the battle, You gave me a melody of breakthrough!

(Psalm 42:8)

Let music rise where mourning tried to linger!

680.

Father, I thank You! The last time I cried in pain was the last time. You rewrote my nights, restructured my body, and renewed my praise.

Let this fire never end. Let this glory never fade. Let this testimony never be replaced.

You are my Healer. You are my Keeper. You are my Forever King!

Hallelujah!

681.

Jesus, the Glory in My Bones, I thank You that my structure is now strength, and my marrow is miracle-filled!

(Ezekiel 37:5)

Let every bone carry Your glory daily!

682.

The God Who Commands Health, I thank You that every organ in me responds to Your voice — not to symptoms!

(Deuteronomy 28:1–2)

Let obedience to glory be permanent in my system!

683.

The One Who Covers My Days, I thank You that no attack can reach me — my years are already marked by praise!

(Psalm 91:16)

Let long life shout thanksgiving in every season!

684.

The One Who Took My Place, I thank You for carrying my weakness so I can now carry worship with power!

(Isaiah 53:4–5)

Let praise rise where pain once ruled!

685.

Jesus, the Fire That Keeps Me, I thank You that even when life tries to shake me, Your presence steadies me with glory!

(Psalm 16:8)

Let my foundation be fireproof forever!

686.

The God Who Marks My Bloodline, I thank You that disease will not enter my children, nor return to my future!

(Exodus 12:13)

Let the blood of Jesus be the generational seal!

687.

The Shield Around My Sleep, I thank You for healing me while I rested — now I rise with new power and peace!

(Psalm 3:5)

Let rest always be restoration from this day forward!

688.

The Giver of Supernatural Health, I thank You that I don't just recover — I exceed human expectation!

(Ephesians 3:20)

Let my life redefine what healing looks like!

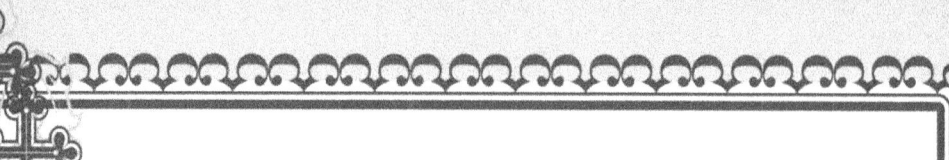

689.

The Fire on My Generations, I thank You that my lineage will never know the diseases that afflicted my past!

(Deuteronomy 7:15)

Let fire stand between then and now forever!

690.

The One Who Commands My Wholeness, I thank You that no residue, no delay, no disturbance can remain!

(Luke 8:48)

Let wholeness echo in my life every day!

691.

Jesus, the One Who Wipes the Tears, I thank You that You've replaced mourning with miracles and silence with songs!

(Revelation 21:4)

Let joy overflow where grief used to live!

692.

The One Who Baptized Me in Fire, I thank You that my entire system is now saturated in glory!

(Luke 3:16)

Let the baptism of fire remain unquenchable!

693.

The Great Deliverer, I thank You that bondage is now memory, and liberty is now my lifestyle!

(Psalm 18:2)

Let freedom roar louder than my past battles!

694.

The God of Forward Only, I thank You that I will never go back to affliction — healing is my direction forever!

(Philippians 3:13–14)

Let progress be my new address!

695.

Jesus, the Song of My Soul, I thank You that my heart now beats to the rhythm of Your glory!

(Psalm 40:3)

Let every beat declare: the Lord has done it!

696.

The One Who Speaks Over My Body, I thank You that Your voice cancelled every whisper of relapse!

(Psalm 29:4)

Let only Your decree stand forever!

697.

The Fire in My Testimony, I thank You that when I speak, devils tremble, and faith is stirred!

(Revelation 12:11)

Let my testimony set others on fire!

698.

The One Who Rebuilds Ruins, I thank You that every scar is now strength, every tear now a torch!

(Isaiah 61:4)

Let former pain fuel future purpose!

699.

The God Who Finishes With Glory, I thank You that You didn't leave me halfway — You completed me with fire!

(Ecclesiastes 3:14)

Let Your perfection echo in every cell of my body!

700.

Father, I thank You! You healed me. You taught me. You lifted me. You clothed me in fire. And now, I walk as proof that the blood still works!

Let every step I take be worship. Let every breath I breathe be warfare. Let every word I speak carry flame.

Sickness is finished. Healing is forever. Glory is rising.

Hallelujah to Jesus, my Victory!

701.

Jesus, the Rock That Cannot Be Moved, I thank You that my healing is immovable, unshakable, and rooted in eternal fire!

(Psalm 62:2)

Let no voice uproot what You've established!

702.

The One Who Called Me Whole, I thank You that Your declaration over me cannot be reversed — I am healed!

(Mark 5:34)

Let Your verdict echo forever in my story!

703.

The God Who Restores in Full, I thank You that no part of me is left unrepaired — physically, emotionally, spiritually!

(Jeremiah 30:17)

Let total recovery define my legacy!

704.

The Fire That Walks With Me, I thank You that in every season forward, I walk in fire, not fear!

(Daniel 3:25)

Let the flame of Your presence go ahead of me!

705.

Jesus, the Overthrower of Darkness, I thank You that no shadow of sickness can survive in Your light!

(John 1:5)

Let divine light blaze through every generation after me!

706.

The Lord of the Finish Line, I thank You that I will finish strong, healthy, and on fire for You — nothing missing!

(2 Timothy 4:7)

Let my ending be louder than my beginning!

707.

The God of Glory Encounters, I thank You for turning affliction into a platform where glory now dwells!

(2 Corinthians 4:17)

Let my testimony carry fire into every room!

708.

The One Who Redeems With Fire, I thank You that my time, strength, and purpose have all been restored with holy fire!

(Joel 2:25–26)

Let divine restoration overflow without limits!

709.

The Eternal Praise-Worthy King, I thank You for writing healing into my DNA — it cannot be undone!

(Psalm 103:3–5)

Let every generation after me inherit this flame!

710.

The One Who Destroys the Destroyer, I thank You for destroying the destroyer — and burning every backup plan of hell!

(Exodus 12:23)

Let no strategy of the enemy survive this glory!

711.

Jesus, the Voice That Shakes Foundations, I thank You that every root of disease collapsed when You spoke!

(Psalm 29:4)

Let Your voice continue to thunder over my body!

712.

The God Who Elevates After Affliction, I thank You that the place of pain has become the platform of praise!

(Psalm 66:12)

Let my promotion carry fire and testimony!

713.

The One Who Destroys the Snare, I thank You that every hidden trap of affliction has been burned beyond recognition!

(Psalm 124:7)

Let my escape be permanent and public!

714.

The Breaker of Resistance, I thank You that no stubborn condition could resist Your glory — You shattered every wall!

(Micah 2:13)

Let the testimony be unstoppable!

715.

The God of Permanent Peace, I thank You that there will be no relapses, no returns, and no residue!

(Nahum 1:9)

Let divine finality surround my healing forever!

716.

Jesus, the Eternal King, I thank You for healing that does not expire — what You did remains done forever!

(Ecclesiastes 3:14)

Let glory be my lifelong covering!

717.

The One Who Opens Rivers in Dry Places, I thank You for flooding my life with miracles where they said there was no hope!

(Isaiah 43:19)

Let every desert now bloom with divine praise!

718.

The Lord of Fire and Wind, I thank You that the wind of Heaven and the fire of glory have replaced every storm of affliction!

(Acts 2:2–3)

Let supernatural weather surround my days!

719.

The One Who Restores My Balance, I thank You that You realigned every nerve, bone, and system into perfection!

(Luke 13:13)

Let uprightness and wholeness testify forever!

720.

Father, I thank You! From the pit to the platform, from affliction to acceleration, from weeping to worship — You did it!

Let every breath, every step, and every moment carry praise and power.

This healing is generational. This fire is eternal. This testimony is indestructible.

Hallelujah to the One who reigns and restores!

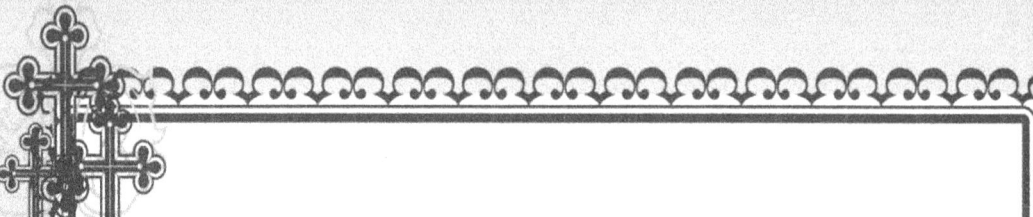

721.

Jesus, the Resurrection in My Blood, I thank You for giving life to every cell, organ, and fiber — nothing dead remains!

(Romans 8:11)

Let resurrection power keep flowing daily!

722.

The One Who Seals With Fire, I thank You that this healing cannot be undone, erased, or reversed!

(Ephesians 1:13)

Let the flame of finality burn forever!

723.

The Banner Over My Body, I thank You that the only name on me now is VICTORY!

(Song of Solomon 2:4)

Let the flag of healing wave across every year ahead!

724.

The Glory That Covers My Past, I thank You that my former affliction has no voice, no sting, no access!

(Isaiah 43:18–19)

Let only Your glory be remembered in my story!

725.

The Fire That Reaches Generations, I thank You that my children and their children shall walk in the fire that healed me!

(Isaiah 59:21)

Let this flame become generational inheritance!

726.

The One Who Walked Me Out, I thank You for holding my hand and leading me step by step into wholeness!

(Psalm 18:36)

Let divine steps continue to lead my life!

727.

The God Who Called Me Out of the Tomb, I thank You for calling me by name — and restoring more than I lost!

(John 11:43)

Let my name be known in hell as untouchable!

728.

The Rock That Cannot Be Moved, I thank You that healing is now my foundation — I will not be shaken!

(Psalm 62:6)

Let divine stability reign forever!

729.

Jesus, the One Who Poured Oil on My Wounds, I thank You for treating me tenderly and restoring me fiercely!

(Luke 10:34)

Let Your oil continue to flow without end!

730.

Father, I thank You! Every affliction has turned into an altar. Every struggle has become a song. Every scar is now a story of glory.

Let the fire of this healing fuel others. Let the light of this miracle shine beyond me. Let my entire being scream: "Look what the Lord has done!"

Hallelujah to the God of glory, forever!

731.

Jesus, my Faithful Witness, I thank You that You stood in the courtroom of Heaven and declared me healed with Your blood!

(Revelation 1:5)

Let the record stand — case closed forever!

732.

The One Who Brings Me Into Wealth and Health, I thank You that affliction is no longer my identity — glory is!

(Deuteronomy 8:18)

Let wholeness and purpose now walk hand in hand!

733.

The Voice That Created My Body, I thank You for commanding every part of me into divine alignment — nothing missing!

(Genesis 1:26)

Let the original blueprint of Heaven remain!

734.

The God Who Wages War With Fire, I thank You that You answered sickness with judgment and affliction with holy wrath!

(Psalm 18:8–14)

Let every enemy of health remain ashes forever!

735.

The One Who Released Me From Captivity, I thank You for breaking every invisible chain and unspoken bondage!

(Isaiah 61:1)

Let liberty echo from my lungs every day!

736.

Jesus, the Fire in My Bloodline, I thank You that what plagued generations before me has now ended with me!

(Exodus 12:13)

Let fire mark this turning point for eternity!

737.

The One Who Keeps Me From Falling, I thank You for holding me when I thought I had nothing left!

(Jude 1:24)

Let Your grip keep my victory secure!

738.

The Strengthener of the Weak, I thank You that even when my body felt like giving up, You surged me with fire!

(Isaiah 40:29)

Let new strength rise every morning like the sun!

739.

The God Who Speaks in Fire, I thank You that one word from You silenced months of pain, doubt, and confusion!

(Psalm 29:7)

Let every report bow to Your decree forever!

740.

Father, I thank You! No system failed. No cell rebelled. No condition survived. No devil prevailed.

This victory is signed in blood, soaked in praise, and sealed with glory.

Let the flame of thanksgiving burn louder than affliction ever did.

Jesus is Lord over my body — forever!

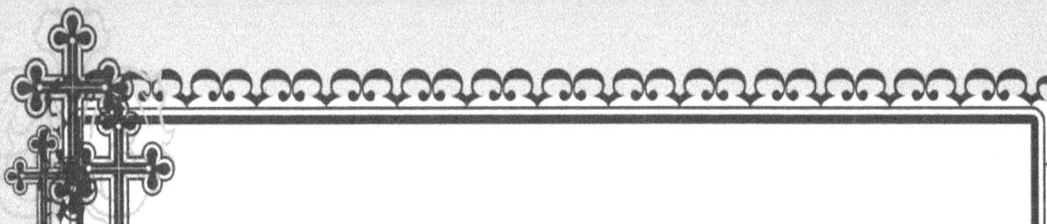

741.

Jesus, my Deliverer from Destruction, I thank You for pulling me out of the valley of disease and placing me in the palace of praise!

(Psalm 103:4)

Let my healing story glorify You forever!

743.

The Giver of Covenant Strength, I thank You that weakness is not my portion — supernatural stamina is!

(Deuteronomy 33:25)

Let my days be marked by fire-filled endurance!

744.

Jesus, the One Who Stood in My Place, I thank You that affliction touched You so it could never touch me again!

(Isaiah 53:5)

Let Your sacrifice speak eternally in my body!

745.

The Restorer of All Things, I thank You for giving back what I didn't even realize I lost in the battle!

(Joel 2:25)

Let the refund of glory continue to overflow!

746.

The Voice That Overwrites Reports, I thank You that what You said about me is louder than any lab result!

(Isaiah 53:1)

Let the scroll of Heaven replace every earthly file!

752.

Lord, I thank You that Your voice shakes the mountains of sickness and levels the hills of affliction!

(Nahum 1:5)

Praise to the Mountain-Moving God!

747.

The God Who Fights Until the End, I thank You that You didn't stop halfway — You finished my healing in full!

(John 19:30)

Let no part be left undone — ever again!

748.

The Fire That Seals My Temple, I thank You that no stranger can enter what You've sanctified with holy flame!

(1 Corinthians 6:19)

Let my body be a no-go zone for affliction forever!

749.

The One Who Dances Over My Testimony, I thank You that You rejoice over me with healing songs and songs of deliverance!

(Zephaniah 3:17)

Let Heaven's joy surround my life daily!

750.

Father, I thank You! I didn't just survive — I was resurrected. I didn't just recover — I was rebuilt. I didn't just heal — I was filled with fire.

Let this body serve You. Let this testimony exalt You. Let every breath declare: Jesus did this!

Hallelujah to the King who makes affliction bow!

751.

Jesus, the One Who Rested and Rose, I thank You that every resting moment now carries resurrection glory in my bones!

(Luke 24:6)

Let my sleep, my strength, and my schedule reflect Your fire!

752.

The God Who Erased My Shame, I thank You that where affliction once embarrassed me, You've now crowned me with honor!

(Isaiah 61:7)

Let royalty replace every label of weakness!

753.

The Voice That Turns Weeping Into Worship, I thank You for rewriting my midnight cries into morning miracles!

(Psalm 30:5)

Let joy be louder than every tear I once cried!

754.

The Lord Who Makes Me Laugh Again, I thank You for restoring the joy I thought I'd lost forever!

(Genesis 21:6)

Let laughter flood every space where sorrow once lived!

755.

The Fire That Consumes Delay, I thank You that healing didn't just come — it came right on time and burned every hindrance!

(Isaiah 60:22)

Let divine timing be my signature forever!

756.

The God Who Removes Labels, I thank You that "sick" is no longer my name — "healed, anointed, chosen" is who I am!

(Isaiah 62:2)

Let divine identity stand for generations to come!

757.

Jesus, the Key of David, I thank You for unlocking doors to healing, purpose, and fire — and shutting doors behind me for good!

(Revelation 3:7)

Let the right doors remain open forever!

758.

The Lord Who Touched the Leper, I thank You that You touched what man avoided — and made it glorious again!

(Mark 1:41)

Let divine boldness define my healing story!

759.

The One Who Walks in the Fire With Me, I thank You that affliction didn't destroy me — it introduced me to deeper glory!

(Daniel 3:25)

Let fire forge my praise into power!

760.

Father, I thank You! You didn't just visit me — You dwelled with me. You didn't just heal me — You filled me. You didn't just restore me — You redefined me.

Let my body be a billboard of Your glory. Let my life be proof that Jesus still heals.

Let my thanksgiving be eternal. Let my healing be generational. Let my altar burn forever. Hallelujah!

761.

Jesus, the God of Divine Closure, I thank You for ending every unresolved health battle with one word: healed!

(Mark 5:34)

Let no chapter be reopened — this story is sealed in glory!

762.

The Lord Who Carries My Burdens, I thank You for lifting what was too heavy and replacing it with rest and fire!

(Matthew 11:28–30)

Let every day carry the rhythm of strength!

763.

The One Who Writes My Days, I thank You that long life is not just a promise — it's my daily reality in fire and praise!

(Psalm 91:16)

Let every hour glorify the Healer who lives in me!

764.

The God of Supernatural Exchange, I thank You for trading my pain for power, my weakness for worship, and my sorrow for songs!

(Isaiah 61:3)

Let this exchange speak through generations!

765.

Jesus, the Lord of Hosts, I thank You for dispatching fire-charged angels to defend my health night and day!

(Psalm 34:7)

Let angelic fire circle my home, my body, my destiny!

766.

The One Who Made Me Whole, I thank You that wholeness is my new baseline — I am not recovering, I am complete!

(Luke 17:19)

Let nothing be missing, nothing be broken ever again!

767.

The God Who Keeps My Breath, I thank You that every breath now praises You, not pain!

(Psalm 150:6)

Let the air in my lungs remain glory-filled forever!

768.

Jesus, the Fire That Fills the Temple, I thank You that my body is no longer a target — it is a throne room!

(1 Corinthians 6:19)

Let sickness see this temple and run in fear!

769.

The Breaker of All Delay, I thank You that my days of "not yet" are over — You have done it now and forever!

(Isaiah 60:22)

Let suddenness surround every testimony!

770.

Father, I thank You! You rewrote my timeline, my testimony, and my entire identity. No voice of doubt can reverse what You've declared.

Let the sound of my healing never grow quiet. Let the altar of thanksgiving in my soul never burn out.

You are the fire in my blood. The name in my lungs. The glory in my story. Hallelujah to Jesus forever!

771.

Jesus, the One Who Fills My Frame, I thank You that no part of me is empty — strength flows through every system!

(Psalm 138:3)

Let every cell vibrate with divine vitality!

772.

The God of Irreversible Healing, I thank You that no enemy can reverse what You have already settled in fire!

(Ecclesiastes 3:14)

Let the seal of Heaven remain unbreakable!

773.

The Giver of Holy Boldness, I thank You that I don't fear recurrence, relapse, or return — I walk in fire-fed faith!

(2 Timothy 1:7)

Let boldness be my healing shield!

774.

The One Who Watches Over My Word, I thank You that my declarations have become flames that burn down opposition!

(Jeremiah 1:12)

Let my words remain fire-lit and faith-filled!

775.

Jesus, the Master of My Temple, I thank You that this body now glorifies You — no more invaders, only Your presence!

(Romans 12:1)

Let this vessel radiate Your glory daily!

776.

The Refiner of My Journey, I thank You that affliction didn't destroy me — it purified me into pure gold!

(Malachi 3:3)

Let the shine of healing never fade!

777.

The Architect of Wholeness, I thank You for rebuilding every torn-down place into a fortress of praise and strength!

(Isaiah 58:12)

Let the foundation of my body remain fire-forged!

778.

The God Who Thunders Over My Enemies, I thank You for scattering every assignment of affliction with one sound from Heaven!

(Psalm 18:13–14)

Let thunder keep responding to my thanksgiving!

779.

The Fire That Fills My Generations, I thank You that what You started in me shall continue in my children and beyond!

(Psalm 112:2)

Let generational healing be our family fire!

780.

Father, I thank You! You lit a fire that sickness cannot touch. You planted glory where pain once ruled. You turned weeping into weapons.

Let this altar never run cold. Let this body forever testify. Let every part of me shout: "It was the Lord who healed me!"

Hallelujah to the God of eternal fire and healing!

781.

Jesus, the God of Divine Finality, I thank You that You didn't just start the miracle — You finished it with fire!

(John 19:30)

Let every part of me remain under Your completed work!

782.

The Fire That Burns Backward, I thank You for reaching into my past and healing wounds I never knew I carried!

(Joel 2:25)

Let no history survive Your holy flame!

783.

The One Who Dismantles Demonic Structures, I thank You for destroying the spiritual systems that sustained my affliction!

(2 Corinthians 10:4)

Let every altar be broken beyond repair!

784.

The Lord My Light, I thank You that Your presence exposed every shadow and replaced it with glory!

(Psalm 27:1)

Let light reign over my mind, body, and soul!

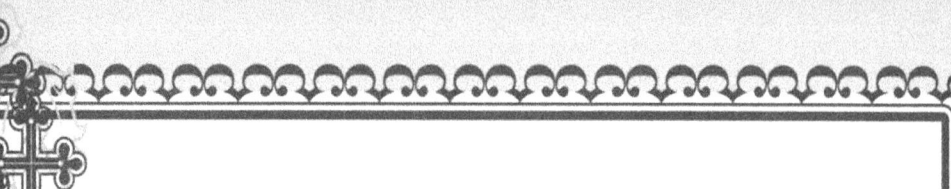

785.

The One Who Rewards Those Who Wait, I thank You that delay was not denial — and my healing has become my harvest!

(Habakkuk 2:3)

Let the fulfillment of Your promise shout louder than the wait!

786.

The Fire on My Bloodline, I thank You that generational sickness has met generational fire — and fire has won!

(Exodus 12:13)

Let the blood still speak and burn through every lineage!

787.

Jesus, the God of Covenant Completion, I thank You that I am not half-healed — I am fully delivered, fully restored, and fully Yours!

(Deuteronomy 7:15)

Let my completeness glorify Your faithfulness!

788.

The One Who Makes Me Whole in Secret, I thank You for healing me privately so I can praise You publicly!

(Matthew 6:6)

Let my private altar produce public glory!

789.

The Lion Who Roars Over My Body, I thank You that no serpent can hiss when the Lion has already roared!

(Amos 3:8)

Let Your roar silence every whisper of fear!

790.

Father, I thank You! I have passed through the valley and come out with victory. What touched me before cannot touch me again.

This is not survival — it is revival. This is not chance — it is covenant. This is not temporary — it is eternal.

Let the fire speak. Let the blood protect. Let the praise remain forever.

Hallelujah to Jesus, the Lord who heals and reigns!

791.

Jesus, the Lord of My Wholeness, I thank You that nothing broken remains — spirit, soul, or body!

(1 Thessalonians 5:23)

Let wholeness define my identity from now on!

792.

The Fire That Shuts Every Door, I thank You for sealing off every entry point sickness once used — permanently!

(Revelation 3:7)

Let no demon find a path into this healed vessel again!

793.

The One Who Makes All Things New, I thank You that I am not just restored — I am redesigned for glory!

(Revelation 21:5)

Let everything about me reflect Heaven's handiwork!

794.

The Shield Over My Destiny, I thank You for defending my purpose from diseases that wanted to interrupt it!

(Psalm 91:4–6)

Let the mission move forward without delay!

795.

Jesus, the Song After the Storm, I thank You that worship now rises from the place pain once lived!

(Psalm 40:3)

Let my melody ignite healing in others!

796.

The One Who Brought Me Through the Fire, I thank You that I emerged without a trace of trauma — only testimony!

(Daniel 3:27)

Let the evidence be fireproof and eternal!

797.

The God Who Declares Me Untouchable, I thank You that affliction has lost permission to knock on my door!

(Galatians 6:17)

Let the mark of Christ be my shield forever!

798.

The One Who Exchanged My History, I thank You that my legacy is now healing, not hurt — power, not pain!

(Isaiah 61:7)

Let my family name be baptized in praise!

799.

The One Who Canceled Every Cycle, I thank You that what used to come back... can't come back anymore!

(Nahum 1:9)

Let the circle of affliction be shattered permanently!

800.

Father, I thank You! I've stepped into the "never again" zone. No more disease. No more dread. No more delay.

This is Your doing — and it is glorious. Let my body remain a sanctuary. Let my story be a sword. Let my voice echo praise for generations.

Hallelujah to Jesus, my Healer, my Defender, my King forever!

801.

Jesus, the Breaker of Chains, I thank You that the cycle is not just broken — it's buried and burned forever!

(Nahum 1:9)

Let no trace of affliction ever rise again!

802.

The One Who Wrote My Recovery, I thank You that this healing isn't guesswork — it was written by Your hand in glory!

(Psalm 139:16)

Let my life read like a book of miracles!

803.

The Fire That Watches the Gate, I thank You that nothing unwanted can enter again — not symptoms, not fear, not sickness!

(Zechariah 2:5)

Let my gates burn with holy resistance!

804.

The God Who Defended Me Silently, I thank You for shielding me from attacks I never even saw coming!

(Psalm 121:7–8)

Let hidden battles continue to end in open praise!

805.

Jesus, my Keeper and Glory, I thank You that my body is no longer a battlefield — it's a throne room!

(Isaiah 60:1)

Let only Your presence dwell here from now on!

806.

The God Who Does the Impossible, I thank You that what doctors gave up on — You picked up and perfected!

(Luke 18:27)

Let every "impossible" bow before Your Name!

807.

The One Who Made Me Laugh Again, I thank You that my laughter is louder than my past pain!

(Genesis 21:6)

Let joy overflow in every room that once knew sorrow!

808.

The Flame That Lights My Future, I thank You that my tomorrow is fire-filled, not fear-filled!

(Jeremiah 29:11)

Let divine expectation govern my journey!

809.

The Blood That Sealed My Healing, I thank You that the price was paid in full — nothing owed, nothing missing!

(Hebrews 9:12)

Let the blood still speak over my life daily!

810.

Father, I thank You! We are almost there — the fire has not faded, and the glory has only increased.

Let my thanksgiving grow louder with every breath. Let every cell continue to testify. Let every step declare: "The Lord has done this!"

Hallelujah to the One who heals completely and forever!

811.

Jesus, the King Who Restores, I thank You for restoring me better than before — stronger, wiser, and filled with fire!

(Joel 2:25)

Let my restoration speak louder than my struggle!

812.

The One Who Fills My Cup, I thank You that I overflow in praise, power, and perfect health!

(Psalm 23:5)

Let this overflow never end — glory to glory!

813.

The God Who Wipes Every Tear, I thank You for drying my sorrow and replacing it with songs of strength!

(Revelation 21:4)

Let joy dance where mourning once stood!

814.

The Fire That Burns All Traces, I thank You that there's no evidence I was ever bound — only testimony that I was delivered!

(Daniel 3:27)

Let fire erase the record, but amplify the praise!

815.

Jesus, the One Who Made Me Fireproof, I thank You that sickness cannot stick, and torment cannot return!

(Luke 10:19)

Let divine immunity be my daily defense!

816.

The Breaker of History, I thank You that generational sickness stopped with me — and healing is now our heritage!

(Galatians 3:13–14)

Let this new chapter be written in power!

817.

The Glory That Covered My Nakedness, I thank You that shame has been replaced with double honor and fire!

(Isaiah 61:7)

Let royalty be seen where pain once ruled!

818.

The One Who Speaks With Authority, I thank You that You didn't negotiate with disease — You commanded it to leave!

(Mark 1:25)

Let every other voice remain silent under Your Word!

819.

The Thunder That Cleared My Path, I thank You that You went ahead of me and shattered every stronghold!

(Psalm 29:3–9)

Let divine sound surround my steps forever!

820.

Father, I thank You! You rewrote my name. You cleared my record. You covered me in fire. You called me healed — and now I call You faithful.

Let my thanksgiving be fuel for generations. Let my healing spark healing in others. Let my praise set the atmosphere on fire.

Hallelujah to the God of wonders, forever!

821.

Jesus, the Flame That Seals, I thank You that what You've healed can never be reopened — not by time, trauma, or enemy!

(Isaiah 22:22)

Let finality mark every part of my testimony!

822.

The God Who Sits in the Fire, I thank You that You purified me without burning me — and refined me without losing me!

(Malachi 3:3)

Let the gold shine and the fire keep burning!

823.

The One Who Lifts the Dust, I thank You for picking me up from the ashes and setting me among fire-filled testimonies!

(Psalm 113:7–8)

Let my elevation speak of Your compassion and power!

824.

Jesus, the One Who Drew Near, I thank You for stepping into my situation with glory, not just sympathy!

(Mark 1:41)

Let divine proximity define every miracle moving forward!

(Almost to 900! Still heavy with fire and names — continuing...)

825.

The Restorer of Rhythm, I thank You that my heartbeat, my breathing, my energy — all now follow Heaven's rhythm!

(Acts 17:28)

Let divine order be my daily experience!

826.

The God Who Turned the Page, I thank You that my life is no longer a story of survival — but revival and testimony!

(Isaiah 43:18–19)

Let this new chapter be written in unending fire!

827.

The Lord My Fire, I thank You that You didn't just fix me — You set me ablaze with praise!

(Hebrews 12:29)

Let this fire light up nations and generations!

828.

The One Who Canceled Every Accusation, I thank You that no voice of darkness can speak again over my body!

(Colossians 2:14–15)

Let Your blood keep silencing my enemies!

829.

The Lion Over My Destiny, I thank You for roaring when I was too weak to speak — and driving fear far away!

(Amos 3:8)

Let the sound of Heaven reign in my atmosphere!

830.

Father, I thank You! The war is over. The pain is gone. The door is shut. The fire is rising.

You have done what no one else could do — and I will never stop declaring: "This is the Lord's doing, and it is marvelous in my eyes!"

Let praise rise. Let healing roar. Let fire speak. Hallelujah to the King forever!

831.

Jesus, the One Who Shuts the Mouth of the Accuser, I thank You that every accusation against my healing is silenced by Your blood!

(Revelation 12:10–11)

Let Your finished work silence the voice of doubt forever!

832.

The God Who Redeemed My Time, I thank You for restoring the years I lost in weakness with days of strength and overflow!

(Joel 2:25)

Let restoration echo in every hour moving forward!

833.

The One Who Fights What I Can't See, I thank You for clearing my path of traps I never knew were set!

(Psalm 91:3)

Let divine defense surround me in every dimension!

834.

The Fire on My Family Tree, I thank You for burning every generational curse and planting new roots of fire and favor!

(Galatians 3:13)

Let glory become our new bloodline signature!

835.

Jesus, the Captain of My Destiny, I thank You that healing was part of Your plan — and now, so is praise!

(Hebrews 12:2)

Let my journey declare the purpose of Your power!

836.

The Healer of My Emotions, I thank You for healing not only my body — but the memories and the moments that broke me!

(Psalm 147:3)

Let joy take the place of every silent wound!

837.

The God Who Took My Shame, I thank You that no whisper of guilt, weakness, or "what if" can stick to me now!(Isaiah 61:7)

Let honor shout louder than what once haunted me!

838.

The One Who Wrote My Future, I thank You that no sickness can edit what You've already sealed in fire! (Psalm 139:16)

Let every year ahead be soaked in healing purpose!

839.

The Flame That Cleansed the Temple, I thank You that every corner of my being is purified and possessed by Your glory!

(2 Chronicles 7:1)

Let nothing unholy find room here ever again!

840.

Father, I thank You! You've lit a fire that sickness cannot survive. You've written a testimony that fear cannot touch.

Let the rest of my life burn with worship, glow with strength, and roar with the sound of victory.

The battle is over. The blood has won. Jesus is Lord forever!

841.

Jesus, the One Who Finished the Assignment, I thank You that no unfinished healing remains — it is done, sealed, and burning with glory!

(John 19:30)

Let my life remain a complete testimony forever!

842.

The God Who Renames and Rebuilds, I thank You that I am no longer called afflicted — I am called restored, honored, healed, and fire-marked!

(Isaiah 62:2–4)

Let my new name echo in Heaven and on Earth!

843.

The One Who Defeated the Grave, I thank You that even death bowed to You — so no disease can ever stand!

(1 Corinthians 15:55–57)

Let resurrection power keep flowing in me!

844.

The Fire That Transforms Weakness Into Strength, I thank You that what broke me now builds me, and what hurt me now fuels my worship!

(2 Corinthians 12:9)

Let Your power continue to rest upon me in fire!

845.

The God of Fresh Oil, I thank You that I'm not just restored — I'm renewed, refueled, and overflowing!

(Psalm 92:10)

Let this oil never run dry in my life again!

846.

The One Who Covers Me in Glory, I thank You for replacing rags of weakness with robes of fire and joy!

(Isaiah 61:3)

Let beauty remain where heaviness used to sit!

847.

Jesus, the Architect of My Praise, I thank You that every part of me now exists to worship You!

(Psalm 103:1–5)

Let my praise be louder than any former pain!

848.

The Lord Who Builds Without Flaws, I thank You that my body has been rebuilt in fire — perfectly, powerfully, permanently!

(Ecclesiastes 3:14)

Let this new foundation never be shaken!

849.

The Flame That Dances Over My Future, I thank You that my days ahead are covered in laughter, strength, and supernatural light!

(Proverbs 4:18)

Let my steps shine brighter with every testimony!

850.

Father, I thank You! You wrote the ending. You won the war. You called me out. You crowned me whole. You covered me with praise.

Let my legacy shout louder than my wounds. Let my life burn as proof. Let my body live as an altar. Let my voice never stop saying:

HALLELUJAH!

851.

Jesus, the One Who Carried Me, I thank You for lifting me when I couldn't stand — and walking me into fire-filled freedom!

(Isaiah 46:4)

Let every step forward carry a footprint of glory!

852.

The God Who Rebuilds With Glory, I thank You that my restoration came with fire, not just function — I am not just well, I am whole!

(Haggai 2:9)

Let the glory of my latter days testify forever!

853.

The Flame That Protects My Borders, I thank You that no more attacks will come near — Your fire is my defense!

(Zechariah 2:5)

Let every gate of my life burn with holy protection!

854.

The One Who Heals Deep Places, I thank You for restoring what no doctor could see and what no medicine could touch!

(Jeremiah 33:6)

Let deep glory continue to fill every hidden place!

855.

The God Who Crowns Me With Lovingkindness, I thank You for removing ashes and placing honor where sorrow once sat!

(Psalm 103:4)

Let dignity dress my life from this day forward!

856.

The One Who Surprises Me With Mercy, I thank You for showing up when I least expected — and leaving a testimony no one can deny!

(Psalm 136:23–24)

Let Your mercy keep multiplying in my life!

857.

Jesus, the Lord of New Beginnings, I thank You that my story didn't end in affliction — it began in fire!

(Isaiah 43:19)

Let every chapter ahead drip with miracle oil!

858.

The Defender of My House, I thank You that sickness will never cross my threshold again — this house is marked by the blood!

(Exodus 12:23)

Let fire rest on my roof, my children, and my future!

859.

The King Who Sat With Me in the Fire, I thank You for not just delivering me — but dwelling with me in the process!

(Daniel 3:25)

Let Your presence never depart from my praise!

860.

Father, I thank You! My days of delay are over. My nights of torment are finished. My altar is lit. My song is louder. My healing is sealed.

Let all of me forever shout: "This is what the Lord has done!"

Let the nations hear it. Let the devil regret it. Let Heaven be praised.

HALLELUJAH!

861.

Jesus, the Flame in My Legacy, I thank You that this fire is not just mine — it will light my children, my household, and my generations!

(Psalm 11`2:2–3)

Let generational glory rise from this testimony!

862.

The God Who Cancels Every Curse, I thank You that every spoken word of infirmity has been reversed by Your blood!

(Galatians 3:13)

Let the curse be buried — and covenant stand forever!

863.

The Lord Who Guards My Gate, I thank You that my body is no longer an open door — it's a fortress of praise!

(Psalm 24:7–9)

Let nothing enter except what You've allowed!

864.

The One Who Answers With Sudden Power, I thank You that my long wait ended with one move from Heaven!

(Isaiah 48:3)

Let sudden healing trigger sudden promotion!

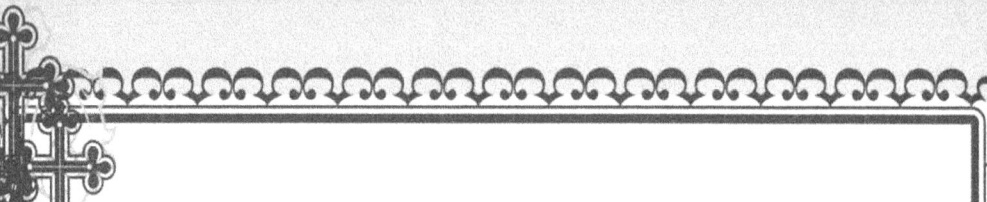

865.

The Restorer of the Weak, I thank You that I no longer walk tired — I walk in divine rhythm and fire-fueled endurance!

(2 Corinthians 12:9)

Let weakness be gone and power overflow forever!

866.

The Fire That Tells My Story, I thank You that even when I'm silent, my healing speaks volumes!

(Revelation 12:11)

Let my testimony be a trumpet in the spirit realm!

867.

The One Who Pulled Me Out, I thank You for rescuing me from secret struggles and turning them into public praise!

(Psalm 40:2–3)

Let this melody never lose its fire!

868.

Jesus, my Life-Giver, I thank You for giving me back everything that sickness tried to steal — and more!

(John 10:10)

Let my new life glorify You with every breath!

869.

The God of Divine Recompense, I thank You that I don't just walk healed — I walk rewarded!

(Isaiah 61:7)

Let my double portion be evident to every eye!

870.

Father, I thank You! You took the ashes of my pain and formed a pillar of praise. You took the depth of affliction and built a mountain of fire.

Let every breath I take shout Your glory. Let every testimony I share release Your power. Let this thanksgiving never end!

Hallelujah to the God of the fire and the finish!

871.

Jesus, the Banner Over My Recovery, I thank You that Your Name now waves over me like a flag of victory!

(Exodus 17:15)

Let every room I enter see the evidence of deliverance!

872.

The One Who Makes Me Fireproof, I thank You that sickness can't survive around me anymore — Your presence is too hot!

(Daniel 3:27)

Let my life repel disease and attract divine health!

873.

The Lord of Glory, I thank You that You didn't just touch me — You transformed me into a walking sanctuary!

(Isaiah 60:1–2)

Let my body radiate Your light forever!

874.

The One Who Brought Me Out With Evidence, I thank You that healing is not just internal — it's undeniable!

(Psalm 105:37)

Let everyone who sees me see what You have done!

875.

The Master Over Time and Process, I thank You that what would take years in the natural, You did in a moment!

(John 5:9)

Let divine acceleration mark the rest of my life!

876.

The One Who Answered With Glory, I thank You that my request was met with more than I imagined — healing and fire!

(Ephesians 3:20)

Let overflow continue to chase me!

877.

The Shield That Cannot Be Penetrated, I thank You that no future attack can reach me — I'm covered in covenant!

(Psalm 91:4)

Let divine resistance stay wrapped around me!

878.

The Flame That Burned the Record, I thank You that every written diagnosis is erased — and replaced with divine praise!

(Colossians 2:14)

Let the only report left be "The Lord has done it!"

879.

The One Who Brought Me Into Rest, I thank You that stress, panic, and fear have no place in my system again!

(Hebrews 4:9–10)

Let supernatural peace saturate my being daily!

880.

Father, I thank You! This is not a moment — it's a memorial. This is not partial — it is perfect. This is not a story — it's a sign to generations.

Let my days be soaked in glory. Let my voice stay ignited in praise. Let my legacy carry fire until You return.

Hallelujah to the Lamb of God, the Healer of the nations!

881.

Jesus, the One Who Shut the Door Behind Me, I thank You that I will never return to that sickness, diagnosis, or pain!

(Isaiah 22:22)

Let every door You closed remain sealed by fire!

882.

The God Who Changes Seasons, I thank You that affliction is no longer my season — praise is!

(Ecclesiastes 3:1)

Let my new season carry permanent celebration!

883.

The God of Holy Completion, I thank You that You finished this healing and wrote "nothing missing, nothing broken" across my body!

(Ecclesiastes 3:14)

Let divine perfection be my new identity!

884.

The Flame on My Tongue, I thank You that my voice is no longer weak — it's a sword of thanksgiving and glory!

(Psalm 149:6)

Let praise be my language forever!

885.

The One Who Took My Burden, I thank You for lifting the invisible weight I carried — now I move in freedom and fire!

(Matthew 11:28)

Let lightness and liberty reign over me!

886.

Jesus, my Atmosphere of Healing, I thank You that everywhere I go now carries glory, presence, and revival!

(Acts 5:15–16)

Let miracles happen in the shadow of my testimony!

887.

The One Who Rewrote My Song, I thank You that "sick" is no longer in my lyrics — only worship, joy, and power!

(Psalm 40:3)

Let my melody stir healing in others!

888.

The God Who Declared "Enough!", I thank You that You interrupted the enemy's cycle and replaced it with covenant victory!

(Nahum 1:9)

Let affliction never rise again in my body or bloodline!

889.

The Fire That Covers My Children, I thank You that healing is not just my testimony — it's my inheritance for generations!

(Psalm 103:17)

Let my lineage carry fire instead of fear!

890.

Father, I thank You! I walk into the final stretch of this journey not limping — but leaping. Not surviving — but singing. Not guessing — but glorifying.

Let every step carry fire. Let every breath burn with worship. Let every word release healing to the nations.

Hallelujah to Jesus, the God who finishes what He starts!

891.

Jesus, the Lord of My Latter Days, I thank You that every day ahead is better than what I left behind — full of strength, clarity, and praise!

(Haggai 2:9)

Let the rest of my life be drenched in glory!

892.

The Fire That Never Fades, I thank You that healing didn't just visit me — it remains, it reigns, and it spreads!

(Leviticus 6:13)

Let this fire never go out in my body or bloodline!

893.

The One Who Rebukes the Devourer, I thank You that disease will never feast on my health again — I am fire-protected!

(Malachi 3:11)

Let divine fire defend what You've restored!

894.

The God Who Replaces Sorrow With Song, I thank You for teaching me how to dance on the ashes of affliction!

(Isaiah 61:3)

Let joy overflow where grief used to linger!

895.

Jesus, the Voice That Reversed the Verdict, I thank You for speaking life when others expected loss — and turning it into laughter!

(Luke 7:14–15)

Let every room I walk into hear my praise!

896.

The Keeper of My Gates, I thank You for guarding every opening of my life — eyes, ears, breath, and borders!

(Psalm 121:8)

Let no sickness gain entrance again!

897.

The Healer of My Atmosphere, I thank You that even the air around me is charged with power, presence, and praise!

(Acts 5:15)

Let healing break out wherever I go!

898.

The One Who Multiplied My Praise, I thank You that what began in tears now multiplies in testimonies!

(Psalm 126:5–6)

Let my harvest of joy never stop growing!

899.

The God of Irreversible Praise, I thank You that I will never return to the silence of fear — my mouth is forever filled with worship!

(Psalm 34:1)

Let my voice remain a flame that honors You!

900.

Father, I thank You! 1,900 declarations of praise, glory, and healing have been lifted before You.

Let every word be fire. Let every prayer be power. Let every breath be bold. Let every testimony draw others to the Healer.

You have been faithful. You have been glorious. You have been enough.

Hallelujah to the Lamb — the Lion — and the Fire that keeps me burning forever!

901.

Jesus, the Final Verdict, I thank You that no report can stand where You've already ruled in my favor!

(Isaiah 54:17)

Let every false sentence be burned by Your decree!

902.

The One Who Made My Body His Temple, I thank You that my body is now fully Yours — fully holy, fully healed!

(1 Corinthians 6:19)

Let nothing impure step foot in this sanctuary again!

903.

The God Who Gave Me a New Reputation, I thank You that I'm no longer known by my battle, but by my breakthrough!

(Isaiah 62:2)

Let my name be "Healed, Whole, and On Fire!"

904

The Flame in My Future, I thank You that every year ahead is set ablaze with Your promises and overflowing with power!

(Proverbs 4:18)

Let momentum replace memory — fire over fear!

905.

The Song in My Spirit, I thank You that I no longer whisper in weakness — I sing in strength!

(Psalm 40:3)

Let melody and miracle walk hand in hand!

906.

The God of My Permanent Victory, I thank You that relapse is not my portion — revival is!

(Nahum 1:9)

Let this deliverance be permanent, public, and prophetic!

907.

Jesus, the One Who Stopped the Bleeding, I thank You that every cycle is broken and every flow has ceased in glory!

(Mark 5:29)

Let Your touch continue to testify in my life!

908.

The Giver of Divine Strength, I thank You for making me stronger after the storm — not just restored, but rebuilt in glory!

(Isaiah 40:29)

Let supernatural stamina be my everyday experience!

909.

The Architect of Praise, I thank You for building me into a living altar — my testimony is now a tabernacle of glory!

(1 Peter 2:5)

Let incense never stop rising from my lips!

910.

Father, I thank You! The finish line is in sight. The flame is burning higher. The enemy is defeated. And glory is permanent.

Let the fire that healed me become the fire that heals others. Let the praise that saved me become a sound to nations.

You are the God of fire, forever! Hallelujah!

911.

Jesus, the One Who Removed My Sackcloth, I thank You that mourning has ended — praise has taken over!

(Psalm 30:11)

Let joy dress me for the rest of my journey!

912.

The God Who Rewrote My Ending, I thank You that sickness doesn't get the last word — Your mercy does!

(Psalm 136:1)

Let grace write every remaining chapter of my life!

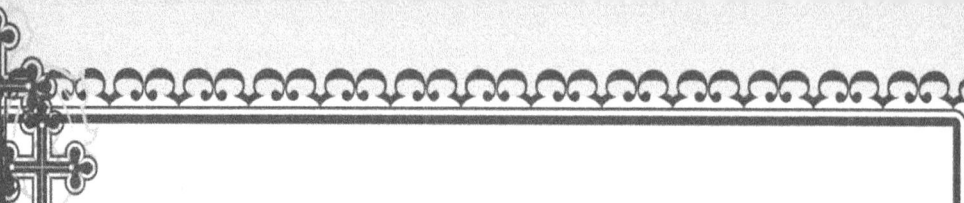

913.

The One Who Sat With Me in the Valley, I thank You for not leaving when others walked away — You healed me in the secret place!

(Psalm 23:4)

Let intimacy with You be my greatest testimony!

914.

The Fire hat Lives in My Bones, I thank You that nothing cold, weak, or fearful can remain in me — only flame!

(Jeremiah 20:9)

Let Your fire become my signature forever!

915.

The Defender of My Promise, I thank You that what You spoke concerning my health came to pass without delay!

(Numbers 23:19)

Let Your faithfulness be shouted for generations!

916.

The Healer of the Nations, I thank You that what You did in me is now flowing into others — my healing is a seed!

(Revelation 22:2)

Let nations drink from this well of testimony!

917.

The One Who Hides Me in Glory, I thank You that sickness can no longer find me — I am hidden in Christ, untouchable!

(Colossians 3:3)

Let divine immunity be my permanent atmosphere!

918.

The God of Glorious Outcomes, I thank You that what looked like the end became the beginning of global fire!

(Romans 8:28)

Let my "almost" be turned into "overflow!"

919.

Jesus, the Lifegiver, I thank You that what tried to take my breath has now birthed my boldest praise!

(Psalm 150:6)

Let my breath always bless the Lord!

920.

Father, I thank You! We are in the final stretch — and You have been nothing but faithful. You turned suffering into fire. Pain into prophecy. Trials into thanksgiving.

Let this moment thunder with praise. Let all of me shout:

HALLELUJAH!

921.

The One Who Burned the Yoke, I thank You that the weight I carried is now ashes — forever destroyed!

(Isaiah 10:27)

Let yokes never return where oil has overflowed!

922.

The Flame That Ignited My Family, I thank You that healing didn't stop with me — it spread through my house like holy wildfire!

(Joshua 24:15)

Let fire be our family's forever inheritance!

923.

The One Who Answered in the Middle of the Night, I thank You that midnight became a miracle moment!

(Acts 16:25–26)

Let my worship always be louder than my warfare!

924.

The Fire That Sealed the Testimony, I thank You that my healing can't be edited — it's written in glory and protected by covenant!

(Psalm 107:20)

Let my story remain untouched by the enemy!

925.

Jesus, the Finisher of My Praise, I thank You that I don't have to wonder anymore — You've done it, and I am whole!

(Philippians 1:6)

Let my thanksgiving finish every future fight!

926.

The One Who Makes My Bones Rejoice, I thank You that even my structure praises You now — I'm healed from the inside out!

(Psalm 51:8)

Let every step, every stretch, every move glorify You!

927.

The God Who Watches Every Cell, I thank You that nothing inside me escapes Your divine supervision!

(Hebrews 4:13)

Let every cell now carry Your fire and order!

928.

The One Who Lights the Lamp, I thank You for igniting joy again — the lamp of my body now glows with strength!

(Proverbs 20:27)

Let darkness never dim my light again!

929.

The Banner That Cannot Be Removed, I thank You that "HEALED BY JESUS" is the title now written over my life!

(Isaiah 11:10)

Let this banner be my identity forever!

930.

Father, I thank You! There are only 70 left, but the fire is still rising. I am more whole than I've ever been. I am more alive than I've ever felt.

Let Your Name receive ALL the glory. Let these 2,000 declarations set the world on fire!

Jesus reigns in my body. Hallelujah forever!

931.

Jesus, the Flame on My Future, I thank You that my tomorrow is guarded, guided, and glowing with Your fire!

(Proverbs 4:18)

Let my next season carry more glory than my last!

932.

The One Who Keeps Me Whole, I thank You that this healing is not seasonal — it's sustained by Your Word!

(Psalm 121:7)

Let the covenant of health be unbroken forever!

933.

The Fire That Traveled Through My Generations, I thank You that sickness exited my bloodline and healing took over!

(Psalm 145:4)

Let every child after me inherit praise, not pain!

934.

The One Who Answered in My Weakest Hour, I thank You that when I couldn't shout, You still showed up in fire!

(Isaiah 40:29)

Let Your strength continue where mine ended!

935.

Jesus, the Fire on My Timeline, I thank You that my past is healed, my present is preserved, and my future is promised!

(Jeremiah 29:11)

Let every hour declare Your goodness!

936.

The One Who Lit My Lamp Again, I thank You for restoring vision, purpose, and joy!

(Psalm 18:28)

Let the fire in my eyes never go out again!

937.

The God of Undeniable Miracles, I thank You that this healing cannot be debated — only declared!

(Psalm 126:1–3)

Let my miracle be loud, lasting, and legendary!

938.

The Defender of My Testimony, I thank You that no enemy can edit what Heaven has sealed!

(Revelation 12:11)

Let my story remain untouched by the hands of darkness!

939.

The God Who Speaks in Silence, I thank You that when I heard nothing — You were still working everything!

(Romans 8:28)

Let trust rise every time it seems quiet!

940.

Father, I thank You! I've been through the fire, and now I burn for You. I've walked through the valley, and now I shout on the mountain.

This healing is not private — it's public, prophetic, and permanent. All glory to Jesus forever!

941.

The One Who Breathed on Dry Places, I thank You for reviving organs, systems, and dreams I thought were gone!

(Ezekiel 37:5)

Let resurrection never stop in my story!

942.

The Fire That Guarded My Night, I thank You for protecting me while I slept — and waking me in praise!

(Psalm 3:5)

Let fire surround my midnight and my morning!

943.

Jesus, the Song That Replaced Sighs, I thank You that sorrow turned to singing, and fear turned to flames of worship!

(Psalm 40:3)

Let melody fill the places mourning once lived!

944.

The One Who Raised Me Higher, I thank You that affliction didn't leave me low — You elevated me with fire and honor!

(Psalm 18:48)

Let my praise rise with every step!

945.

The God of Uninterrupted Recovery, I thank You that there were no setbacks — only progress and praise!

(Philippians 1:6)

Let my healing journey stay bathed in grace!

946.

The Builder of My Praise Life, I thank You for teaching me to worship through the storm and win with a whisper!

(Psalm 34:1)

Let my lips never know silence again!

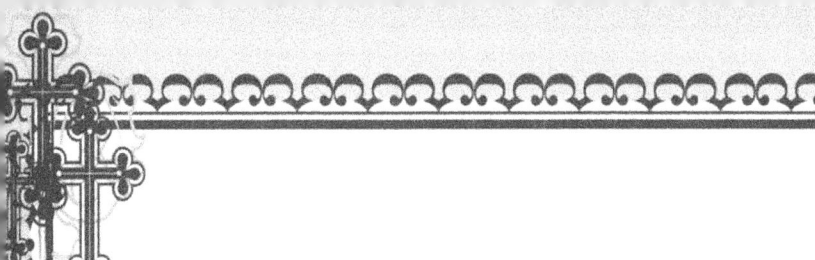

947.

The One Who Finished the Fire Fight, I thank You for not just defeating sickness — but burning its camp to ashes!

(Exodus 15:26)

Let no enemy return to what You have consumed!

948.

The King Who Wrote My Victory, I thank You that my story ends in health, strength, and everlasting fire!

(Psalm 91:16)

Let the pages of my life carry Your Name forever!

949.

The Fire That Cannot Be Hidden, I thank You that even when I try to stay quiet, my healing speaks louder!

(Matthew 5:14–16)

Let my life shine brighter with every step I take!

950.

Father, I thank You! Fifty left — but the fire is stronger. Let every breath shout praise. Let every cell sing testimony. Let every moment magnify Jesus!

This altar of thanksgiving is now eternal. My life is a temple. And my healing is a holy fire!

951.

Jesus, the King Who Never Lost a Battle, I thank You that my healing was never a maybe — it was a guaranteed victory!

(2 Chronicles 20:15)

Let my life remain under Your endless triumph!

952.

The Fire That Walked With Me, I thank You for journeying through every season with me — not once did You let me fall!

(Isaiah 43:2)

Let my gratitude burn brighter than my past pain!

953.

The God Who Answers With Glory, I thank You for not just healing me — but clothing me with beauty, dignity, and praise!

(Isaiah 61:3)

Let glory shine from every part of my life!

954.

The One Who Turned My Cry Into a Call, I thank You that what hurt me now fuels my ministry and mission!

(Genesis 50:20)

Let what was meant for evil continue to produce fire!

955.

Jesus, the Captain of the Last Mile, I thank You that I didn't just begin this healing journey — I finished it with You in glory!

(Hebrews 12:2)

Let every ending declare Your everlasting faithfulness!

956.

The One Who Dances Over My Deliverance, I thank You for rejoicing over me with songs of victory and war cries of love!

(Zephaniah 3:17)

Let my testimony echo in Heaven forever!

957.

The One Who Builds My Legacy, I thank You that this healing will outlive me — it will bless nations, light families, and glorify You!

(Psalm 145:4)

Let my legacy be fire-carved and faith-filled!

958.

The One Who Lit My Voice, I thank You for giving me a sound no devil can silence — praise that roars and healing that speaks!

(Psalm 107:2)

Let my voice remain a flame that fuels others!

959.

The God of the Final Declaration, I thank You that what You said over me still stands: Healed. Delivered. Mine.

(Lamentations 3:37)

Let no other name be spoken but JESUS!

960.

Father, I thank You! These 1,960 declarations have burned through time, torn through darkness, and glorified Your Name.

Let the next 40 finish this fire in power, praise, and forever glory! Let nothing stop the

Hallelujah!

961.

Jesus, the One Who Carried the Cross, I thank You for carrying my sickness on Your shoulders — and exchanging it for strength!

(Isaiah 53:4–5)

Let my praise carry the weight of Your glory now!

962.

The Flame That Cannot Be Contained, I thank You that what You've done in me cannot be hidden — it must be declared!

(Mark 7:36–37)

Let my fire testify even in silence!

963.

The One Who Branded Me With Fire, I thank You that the enemy can't find me anymore — I'm sealed and surrounded!

(Galatians 6:17)

Let the mark of Christ remain visible forever!

964.

The One Who Reversed the Pattern, I thank You that what once repeated has now been replaced with revival!

(Nahum 1:9)

Let fire guard this divine shift forever!

965.

The Glory That Took Over, I thank You that weakness has no space left — Your glory fills every room in me!

(2 Corinthians 4:7)

Let the treasure in this jar shine endlessly!

966.

The One Who Called Me Clean, I thank You for calling me what You created me to be — whole, strong, and fire-filled!

(Luke 5:13)

Let the label "cleansed" never be removed!

967.

The Lord of Divine Exchange, I thank You for replacing my war with worship and my wounds with weapons of praise!

(Isaiah 61:3)

Let my exchange be a testimony for the broken!

968.

The Flame in My Legacy, I thank You that my children and their children will know this altar and build upon it!

(Proverbs 13:22)

Let the generations praise You louder than me!

969.

The God Who Keeps His Word, I thank You that not one prayer has been wasted — You turned every cry into fire!

(Isaiah 55:11)

Let Your promises continue to walk through me!

970.

Father, I thank You! Thirty remain, but the flame has already filled the temple. My healing is not a chapter — it's the whole book.

Let this fire write the conclusion. Let this praise shake the heavens.

Let this Hallelujah never die!

971.

Jesus, the Flame in My Future, I thank You that every day ahead is already lit with promise, peace, and praise!

(Proverbs 4:18)

Let the brightness of my journey glorify You!

972.

The One Who Speaks to Storms, I thank You for calming the violent winds of pain and commanding stillness in my life!

(Mark 4:39)

Let peace reign and praise never cease!

973.

The God of Recompense, I thank You for restoring every lost year, every drained day, every stolen moment!

(Joel 2:25)

Let compensation continue in waves of fire!

974.

The One Who Dwelt in My Battle, I thank You for never leaving me when I cried, questioned, or collapsed!

(Psalm 34:18)

Let intimacy with You be my lifelong anchor!

975.

The One Who Wrote My Ending in Fire, I thank You that I will never end in weakness, only in worship and strength!

(2 Timothy 4:7)

Let my finish glorify You forever!

976.

Jesus, the One Who Deserves All Praise, I thank You for turning my affliction into an anthem of power!

(Psalm 103:1–5)

Let everything in me bless Your holy Name forever!

977.

The One Who Lit My House, I thank You that my home is now covered in glory — affliction shall not enter again!

(Exodus 12:13)

Let divine fire dwell where we live, sleep, and walk!

978.

The Healer of My Hidden Scars, I thank You that even the wounds I never spoke have been wiped away!

(Psalm 147:3)

Let nothing dark remain — only light and liberty!

979.

The God of More Than Enough, I thank You for not just restoring me — but overwhelming me with healing, joy, and peace!

(Ephesians 3:20)

Let abundance be my lifestyle from now on!

980.

Father, I thank You! I stand in the final fire, and I still burn with praise. I am proof that Jesus heals. I am evidence that glory wins.

Let this final stretch shout louder than the storm. Let this moment mark history.

Let my life scream HALLELUJAH!

981.

The One Who Outlasts the Trial, I thank You that You are still here — stronger, closer, and more glorious than ever!

(Hebrews 13:8)

Let my altar burn forever before Your throne!

982.

The One Who Turned Tests Into Fire, I thank You that the tests became fuel — and now my whole life is a furnace of praise!

(James 1:2–4)

Let worship rise from what once hurt me!

983.

The Keeper of My Praise, I thank You that my praise will never fade — it's fireproof and eternal!

(Psalm 34:1)

Let my worship never know silence again!

984.

The God Who Turned Delay Into Display, I thank You for using every waiting moment to build a public altar of power!

(Habakkuk 2:3)

Let patience continue to birth glory!

985.

Jesus, the Fire That Finished My Fight, I thank You that no enemy survived — the war is over and I walk in power!

(Exodus 14:13–14)

Let my enemies remain permanently silenced!

986.

The One Who Made Me a Vessel of Fire, I thank You that I'm not just healed — I'm a living altar!

(Romans 12:1)

Let everything in me serve You forever!

987.

The One Who Spoke the Final Word, I thank You that "HEALED" is the last sentence, and it cannot be edited!

(Isaiah 55:11)

Let Your Word forever speak over my body!

988.

The Flame in My DNA, I thank You that healing now runs through my blood — fire in my cells, fire in my breath!

(Romans 8:11)

Let resurrection remain in my genetic line forever!

989.

The God Who Finishes With Glory, I thank You that this journey ends with praise, with fire, with nations watching!

(Isaiah 60:1–3)

Let Your light be seen in me forever!

990.

Father, I thank You! Ten remain — but the heavens are already shouting. I am Yours. This story is Yours. This body is Yours.

Let the final declarations be crowns before Your throne. Jesus is worthy forever!

991.

Jesus, the Voice That Covered My Valley, I thank You for being louder than every diagnosis, delay, and doubt!

(Psalm 23:4)

Let my valleys become highways of glory!

992.

The One Who Lit a Global Fire, I thank You that this testimony will travel further than affliction ever did!

(Revelation 12:11)

Let fire spread through nations from this altar!

993.

The Lord My Defender, I thank You that I don't fight anymore — I praise while You protect!

(Exodus 14:14)

Let this rest be my inheritance forever!

994.

The God Who Exchanged Ashes for Glory, I thank You for transforming pain into power, and weakness into worship!

(Isaiah 61:3)

Let everyone who sees me glorify the Lord!

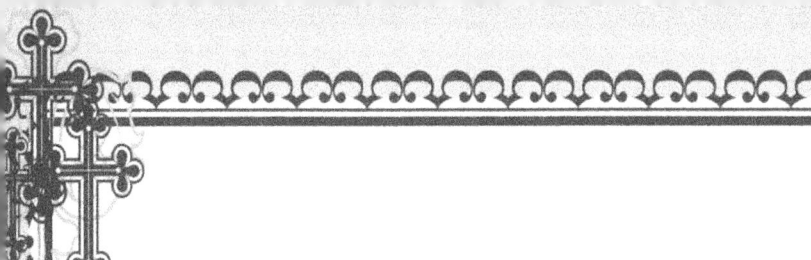

995.

The Healer Who Became My Identity, I thank You that I'm no longer known by pain — but by the power of Jesus Christ!

(Luke 13:12)

Let my name echo in Heaven and silence hell!

996.

Jesus, the One Who Made My Testimony a Tool, I thank You that others will be delivered because of what You did in me!

(2 Corinthians 1:4)

Let this healing become a harvest for others!

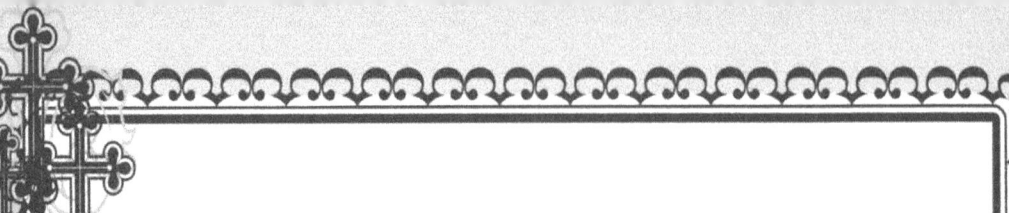

997.

The Flame That Outlasted the Fire, I thank You that Your presence is more powerful than the worst days I've known!

(Isaiah 43:2)

Let my survival be redefined as revival!

998.

The Glory in My Journey, I thank You that every part of this story glorifies You — even the waiting, the crying, the fighting!

(Romans 8:18)

Let nothing be wasted, and everything be worship!

999.

The King Who Gets All the Glory, I thank You that I did not heal myself — it was all You, Jesus!

(Psalm 115:1)

Let the credit stay at the foot of the Cross forever!

1000.

Father, I thank You!

From 1 to 2,000 — every word, every tear, every shout has been for Your glory. You healed me. You carried me. You raised me. You marked me.

Let these 2,000 fire-packed prayers become a sword in the hands of others. Let healing spread like fire. Let nations burn with thanksgiving.

This altar is complete. This covenant is sealed. This praise is forever.

Hallelujah to Jesus — the Healer of my body, the Keeper of my soul, the King of my fire!

With hearts full of gratitude, we bring this first edition to a close. Each prayer within these pages has been a step on the path of thanksgiving, a whisper of praise, and a reflection of faith.

The next edition awaits, and with it, new prayers, renewed hearts, and deeper devotion.
Until then, may the Lord bless you and keep you,
May His face shine upon you and give you peace.

Amen.

Word for the Readers from the Author

Evangelist Tracy C. Moonga

Declarations for the Reader

Make these your daily confession of victory, healing, and fire!

I declare that sickness has no dominion over my body I walk in divine health and total restoration.

I declare that every organ, every cell, and every system in my body is functioning according to God's original design.

I declare that no affliction will return — this healing is permanent and sealed by the blood of Jesus.

I declare that I am a walking altar of fire — wherever I go, healing follows, and devils flee.

I declare that my testimony will ignite others and draw souls into the Kingdom.

I declare that my life, my breath, and my voice will glorify Jesus all my days!

In Jesus' Name — Amen!

Final Reader Declaration

(To be read boldly by the reader as a prophetic activation)

I boldly declare:

I am healed, whole, and sealed by the blood of Jesus.

No weapon formed against my body shall prosper.

No diagnosis, delay, or demonic cycle can rise again.

I walk in divine health, generational healing, and supernatural peace.

This body is a temple.

This voice is a flame.

This life is an altar.

I carry the fire of healing.

I carry the legacy of deliverance.

I carry the name of Jesus.

I will live long.

I will live strong.

And I will burn with praise forever!

Hallelujah — it is done!

Healing Activation Prayer

(To be prayed as a final impartation over the reader)

Father, in the Name of Jesus, I activate healing fire over this reader.

Let Your presence saturate every cell, every bone, every blood vessel.

Let Your glory sweep through every system and flush out every residue of affliction.

Let strength rise, joy overflow, and peace reign.

Let every testimony multiply.

Let every delay be broken.

Let every altar of affliction be consumed by Your fire.

I declare this body untouchable.

This life unshakable.

This praise uncontainable.

May this reader become a carrier of glory — a walking altar of healing and revival.

I call forth their voice, their victory, and their divine assignment in the Name of Jesus.

From today, they shall burn with fire and walk in healing all their days.

Amen and Amen.

Books by Evangelist Tracy C. Moonga

A prophetic healing and deliverance arsenal for this generation:

1. 2000 Fire-Packed Thanksgiving Prayers to Crush Sickness and Defeat the Devil
2. 1000 Atomic Bomb Missiles Against Witchcraft and Evil Altars
3. 2,000 Fire-Packed Thanksgiving Prayers to Crush Sickness and Defeat the Devil
4. 200 Daily Prophetic Personalized Scriptural Declarations for Divine Healing and Long Life
5. Healing in Advance: Prayers of Thanksgiving and Faith
6. The Psalms Arsenal: 365 Personalized Confessions for Spiritual Warfare and Empowerment
7. Fire-Packed Prayers for Spiritual Warfare, Breakthroughs and Deliverance
8. Pleading the Blood of Jesus: Fire-Packed Prayers and Declarations for Healing, Deliverance, and Total Victory
9. Father, I Thank You for Healing
10. Win a Soul for Christ
11. Single With a Purpose
12. Bone of My Bones and Flesh of My Flesh
13. Be the Doer of God's Word in Faith
14. Wounded but Not Defeated: Storms Were Meant to Shape You, Not Break You
15. Seek God First and These Things Shall Be Added to You
16. Don't Miss Eternity: The Call to a Meaningful Life

And more prophetic volumes being birthed under the anointing!

Author's Brand Identity

Evangelist Tracy C. Moonga

Healing Minister | Fire-Prophetic Voice | End-Time Warrior

Soul-Winner with a Divine Assignment to Populate Heaven and Depopulate Hell

Book Cover Bio (Back Cover Ready)

Evangelist Tracy C. Moonga is a fire-filled healing minister, intercessor, and prophetic author called to raise altars of prayer and glory in this generation

She has written over 30+ power-packed books filled with declarations, warfare strategy, and life-changing testimonies.

Healed, called, and ignited by God, she writes from personal encounter — turning affliction into fire and praise.

Her mission: To populate Heaven, depopulate Hell, and bring healing to nations through the Word, fire, and prayer.

Connect with her and discover a library of spiritual weapons for your journ

www.ingramcontent.com/pod-product-compliance
Lightning Source LLC
Chambersburg PA
CBHW041720100526
44583CB00057BA/2996